I0491692

Magnetic Words

The #1 Email Marketing System to Build Lists from Scratch & Craft Irresistible Copywriting

Alina Swanson

© **Copyright 2020 by _____. All right reserved.**

The work contained herein has been produced with the intent to provide relevant knowledge and information on the topic on the topic described in the title for entertainment purposes only. While the author has gone to every extent to furnish up to date and true information, no claims can be made as to its accuracy or validity as the author has made no claims to be an expert on this topic. Notwithstanding, the reader is asked to do their own research and consult any subject matter experts they deem necessary to ensure the quality and accuracy of the material presented herein.

This statement is legally binding as deemed by the Committee of Publishers Association and the American Bar Association for the territory of the United States. Other jurisdictions may apply their own legal statutes. Any reproduction, transmission or copying of this material contained in this work without the express written consent of the copyright holder shall be deemed as a copyright violation as per the current legislation in force on the date of publishing and subsequent time thereafter. All additional works derived from this material may be claimed by the holder of this copyright.

The data, depictions, events, descriptions and all other information forthwith are considered to be true, fair and accurate unless the work is expressly described as a work of fiction. Regardless of the nature of this work, the Publisher is exempt from any responsibility of actions taken by the reader in conjunction with this work. The Publisher acknowledges that the reader acts of their own accord and releases the author and Publisher of any responsibility for the observance of tips, advice, counsel, strategies and techniques that may be offered in this volume.

Table of Contents

Introduction

Why waste a sentence saying nothing? - by Seth Godin.

There is no greater skill than being able to assemble a compelling sales argument. "It is a skill that very few people know of, but once you master it, you'll never have to worry about your business again. You will have the power to generate the highest return on investment for any marketing campaign you invest in. You will have the inside knowledge you need to launch or grow any business you desire. You've heard how the pen is mightier than the sword. You've heard how powerful the words you speak can be. A simple word or two is sometimes enough to completely change your world, and it is this untapped potential of the written and spoken word that is going to take your marketing efforts and skyrocket them to greater heights. It is the power of copywriting combined with the most underrated marketing tool there is - *email marketing.*

Some may say email marketing is dead and not as effective as social media is today, but nothing could be further from the truth. Emails are still one of the best marketing strategies today. Yes, even with the more innovative digital methods. 82% of businesses still use email marketing technology, and you're *six times* more likely to achieve your click-through rate targets with an email campaign than you are from a Tweet. According to HubSpot, everyone dollar spent on email marketing generates returns of 38 dollars. There are other important numbers to keep in mind. Like the fact that 73% of millennials prefer communication from brands to come to them in the form of an email. Email marketing lists are the heart and soul of successful copywriting. They create small, niche audiences that the writer can address directly to deliver a more impactful message. With more than 50% of people in the US check their personal emails up to 10 times daily and 99% of consumers who now have the habit of checking their emails daily too, this is a marketing opportunity you can't afford to pass up. 59% of the survey participants responded that marketing emails had had a big role to play in influencing their purchase decisions.

Email marketing only works if people want to receive the message, and that's where the power of list building comes in. Small and medium-sized businesses understand the importance of list quality. In fact, 66% view it as a bigger factor for success than increasing conversion rates or the size of the list itself. List building is, without a doubt, one of the most important success factors since people are being bombarded by marketing messages from all directions. In 2018 alone, there was a staggering 124.5 billion business emails that were sent and an equally impressive 111.1 billion consumer emails. These are stats no marketer can afford to pass up.

If you've been struggling to get real results through your email marketing campaign, it's because you were probably not sending the *right kind* of emails. The kind of emails with copy that creates an impact. You haven't yet mastered the art of a good copy that is magnetic and captivating enough to turn words into sales. That's where this book comes in. *Magnetic Words* is going to give you the ability that every marketer wishes they had. The ability to get inside people's heads and say things in a way that their messages resonate so well that it compels the reader to take action. Copywriting is a skill that can be learned. Writing email messages that leave your readers feeling like you have a direct link inside their brain, that you know exactly what they've been looking for and how to solve a problem they have is going to be your Midas touch. This is where the magic happens, and it begins with learning the secrets for irresistible copywriting and the secrets of building an email list with loyal, lifelong subscribers.

About the Author

Alina Swanson is a well-known name in the world of digital marketing. She's the creator behind some of the most impressive Ogilvy ads in the UK. She started her career as an intern shortly after graduating from university with a journalism degree. Eventually, her supervisors noticed Alina's uncanny ability to turn words into powerful messages that people want to read. Alina spent more than 15 years at Ogilvy, crafting copywriting campaigns for a vast range of the company's biggest clients. Some of her messages and ads have been recognized and awarded nationally and across an array of industry events. Today, Alina is the owner of her small and niche copywriting agency. She also podcasts on a weekly basis, teaching others how to harness the power of words. Her philosophy is that copy shouldn't try to sell. It should touch the soul of a person, whether in a humorous or an emotional way. *Magnetic Words* is Alina Swanson's first book, sharing her work experience and the copywriting techniques that she developed over the course of her career.

Chapter 1: Building Your Email List

What's the best-kept secret to a great marketing campaign? Two words: Email lists.

If you're still looking for a proven way to drive sales and increase revenue, then building an email list is a tried and true method that is still a favorite marketing technique. *Email marketing is effective and works.* Regardless whether you're a business to consumer (B2C) or in the business to consumer (B2C) market. The fact we cannot ignore is that you're all your customers will likely have some email access, and that is going to be their first resort when they attempt to reach you. There are two main reasons why every business should have a list of customers and leads that it communicates with on a regular basis, and those reasons are:

- So they don't forget about you

- To let them know what is happening and what is new in your business

What Is an Email List?

An email list is essentially a list of people who have signed up to receive emails from you. The most important part here is that *they have given you permission* to contact them through their personal email accounts. This means they actually do want to hear from you. Email lists are managed through a software that allows you to keep your list organized and send out messages to everyone on your list at the same time instead of manually having to do it one by one. This saves you a tremendous amount of time, *and* you'll be able to track which messages were opened, which weren't, and which of your emails were marked as spam.

With email lists, you have the option of creating a general list for all your subscribers or segmenting your email lists based on the different groups you want your emails to go out to. For example, you could create an email list for people who have purchased a specific product, people who are repeat and loyal customers, people who are prospective customers, people who are on the lookout for your next big sale, and so on. An email list can be created based on what your marketing needs and goals are at the time; that's the beauty of this approach. An email list is so important that you need to create this list *first* even before you've started copywriting your material. Why? Because without a specific audience that you're speaking to in mind, you won't be able to craft the perfect content. You need to know who you're talking to, what they want from your business, what is a pain point they're looking to resolve, and how your business can help fill a void in their need. Only when you've got the information on hand can you then begin crafting content that is tailor-made to fit the specific audience, you're trying to reach so your message resonates with them loud and clear.

What makes email marketing so special? Besides collecting important email contact that could be turned into potential paying clients, compared to all the other marketing channels out there, emails still give you the most direct access to your customer. Building an email list would be among the common suggestions and advice you would have been bound to come across if you have been studiously researching what the best marketing methods are, and there's a good reason why. If you are a marketer that is selling a product or service of any kind on your blog, it is imperative that you have an email list or an email newsletter or some sort because it can be a powerful sales tool that you are not taking full advantage of. An email list is a way for you to keep your subscribers updated about the products and services that you're marketing and trying to sell, and more importantly, it alerts them about any new products or services that are now available. If they don't know about it, how can they purchase it? When you've invested that time and effort into creating a message specifically for them, you want to make sure they get that message loud and clear so you, in turn, can get the return on investment you're looking for.

Email marketing is extremely easy to use, and that's why it has become part of every marketer's go-to marketing strategy. An email list can quickly be put together based on demographics, purchase history, customer loyalty, affiliates, prospects, customers who have abandoned their shopping carts halfway, or customers who have signed up specifically for offers and discounts. An email list means more website traffic for you in return, especially if your readers subscribe to your list and keep visiting your blog each time, they get an update about something new that is happening on your site.

Is Email Marketing Still Effective Today?

Despite how dominant social media is in the advertising and marketing scene, no, email marketing is not outdated. Email marketing is only considered poor form when it becomes a mindless barrage of emails being sent to your customers that you end up spamming them in the hopes of getting their attention. This is something you want to avoid because you'll only end up annoying your customers to no end if you send them far too many emails. The only email marketing works like a charm is when it is best used *only to keep your customers informed.*

Not building an email list is one of the biggest mistakes a business could make. There's a misconception around how email lists are not as important, and all the attention is directed toward growing followers or copywriting material in the hopes it's persuasive enough to sell. The focus for a lot of businesses today is how to grow their following on social media in particular. They believe that if they conquer the social media scene, their marketing game is set, but nothing could be further from the truth. There's a big problem with social media channels: *You don't own the communication on those channels.* Even if your followers have liked your page or subscribed to your channel, there's a good chance they do not see a lot of the content you put out there because of the algorithms in place on these channels. That's a problem, but that problem is exactly why email lists are still relevant.

Any business that is operating has an email account. You cannot run a business without it. Anyone with an internet connection has an email. Heck, they may even have more than one email account these days. Our work and our personal lives revolve around technology and communication, and despite the multiple apps and social media sites available out there, the one thing that remains consistent is this: *Everyone with an internet connection has an email account.* Not everyone may have a Facebook account, Instagram, Twitter, Google Plus, LinkedIn, Zoom, or any of the many social channels out there. Even if they did, there's no guarantee they're active users of these platforms. But you can bet that everyone checks their emails at least once a day. As long as our lives revolve around email as a primary form of communication, there will always be a need for email marketing.

There's a lot of content that can be put into your email marketing. In fact, it is probably one of your most customizable marketing options, which is why it is still relevant today as an effective marketing tactic. A lot of businesses tend to get swept up in the idea that social media marketing is the way to go because social media is *everywhere you go.* But you know what? *So are emails.* Customers check their email daily the way they check their social media apps, with one crucial difference: *They take the time to read the emails that they receive.* You could create variety by sometimes sending articles, or links, making announcements, sharing customer testimonials, really the sky's the limit, and the options are anything you want it to be.

Is email marketing and building an email list unnecessary and outdated? Far from it. Despite the growing popularity of social media, email marketing is not going anywhere anytime soon. Email continues to be among the more popular ways that businesses and customers connect with each other directly, and it offers something that social media cannot at this stage: personalizing your messages directly to the person that you're emailing, almost as if you were speaking to them directly.

How Do I Build an Email List from Scratch?

Opt-ins, lead magnets, and freebies. Those three words can be interchangeable, but these are the keywords that matter when you're trying to build your list from scratch. Building an email list requires that your customers give you their email address in exchange for something that you offer. That "something" has to be worth their while or they won't be willing to relinquish their email address just like that. People are sometimes reluctant to give away their email address for fear of being spammed annoying in their inboxes by unwanted emails. Unless there was a good enough incentive and reason for them to do so. Everyone loves to receive a little gift for free, so why not try that tactic to entice your readers to sign up for your newsletter when they visit your website? Depending on the nature of your business, try to provide a giveaway that is going to be something of value to your readers, something they would be excited to receive in their inbox. Perhaps a discount to one of your products or services for example.

You want to make sure that your freebie or lead magnets are juicy enough for them to want to subscribe to your page. Examples of enticing lead magnets or freebies include PDF guides, discounts, free video training, or free audio file. It depends entirely on the nature of your business. No matter what type of format your lead magnet may be in, you want to make sure it is *something your audience wants*. They're not going to subscribe or give you their email address if what you're offering is of little to no value to them. Your content also needs to relate to your business; otherwise, it's not going to make sense to your customers.

Now, once you have your lead magnet or freebie created, these are the next few steps you need to take to collect the emails to create your list:

- **Starting with Who You Know** - The easiest way to start building a list is to start with who you already know. Are there any customers you already keep on file? Do you have a database of emails from any previous marketing campaigns you've run in the past? Start with the information you already have on hand before looking at ways to expand from there. Existing customers must be part of your list, especially if these are loyal customers who have been following your business for a while now.

- **Create A Landing Page** - Your customers need somewhere to go to fill out their name, email address, and any other information you might need. A landing page that is well-constructed is your best chance of achieving better ROIs, and whether they turn into paying customers or not is going to depend entirely on what they see when they land after that "click." A quick rule of thumb to remember when constructing your landing page is, the better your design and copy, the better the conversions you will see.

- **Email Marketing Software** - MailChimp is among the most common types of email marketing software that a lot of marketers use, especially if you're working on a budget. Convert Kit, Drip, Kajabi, Active Campaign, Click Funnels, and Aweber are other examples of great platforms you can consider too. A little research and due diligence are required here to ensure that you are purchasing the best software for your business. Ideally, you want to go for software that will allow you to do tagging and segmentation.

- **Have A Blog** - Blogs offer an added incentive for customers to want to subscribe and drive traffic. A blog lends credibility to your business, especially when it is filled with valuable content. It reinforces the idea that you are an authority in your field. That could be a huge advantage to your business and it will help to drive traffic much faster towards your site. Quality is key to keeping your customers subscribed, and although crafting quality content that adds value might be an extra step to take, it is going to be worth it.

- **Have A Call to Action (CTAs) -** Your marketing goal is to acquire leads. Your CTA should be clear on your website so that it is easy for your customers to understand what they are being led to do. CTAs are a very big part of that marketing goal because a strong CTA is the one that tells your customers and your email readers what action they need to take next.

An effective CTA is one which encourages conversions, downloads, purchases, sign-ups, donations, RSVPs, and more. You've done a good job of convincing your customer thus far; now you just need to reel them in with a strong CTA so that they no longer hesitate to take any action. Use action-oriented words in your CTA (*learn more, read more, sign up now*). Create a sense of urgency, so your audience is prompted to take action.

- **Exit Popups** - Before your customer or prospective customer is about to leave your site, ask them a yes or no question. It's an opportunity to collect their information, even as they are about to leave your page. Pop-ups are annoying, yes, but on some level, they actually do work, especially if the customer is already showing a keen interest in your site and is a frequent visitor. Many sites incorporate the use of pop-ups encouraging customers to sign up for their newsletter or subscribe to their blog. You've seen it if you've visited other websites yourself. Annoying at times, yes, but there is a reason many blogs are using this. Because they work. If they click "yes" to your popup question, you get to capture their email address. Since they're leaving your website anyway, there's no harm in asking them one last time for their email address.

Segmentation Essentials

Sending out emails and regularly corresponding with your customers and leads is great, but it's not enough. Once you've created your email list, segmentation is the next step you want to think about. Segmenting your email list can be a valuable resource, especially since you could potentially generate a lot of great leads from this list that could be turned into paying customers.

An email list is a fantastic marketing tool, *but only if it is used correctly.* Hence the need for segmentation. Sending out the same email to everyone on your list is like playing darts with the blindfold on. Maybe your message might hit the right target, but most likely it won't. List segmentation is the process of taking your email list and then dividing the emails into groups. By diving your customers into groups, it allows you to send more targeted messages. This way, you get to target your customers based on geographical location, age, sex, gender, and other pertinent information you gather from their demographics.

Targeting your messages means you're sending the right message to the *right* group of audiences, which maximizes your chances of converting these leads into paying customers. You won't necessarily send the same generic email out to everyone in your email list if you know it's not going to be as effective. Existing and loyal customers will be looking for a different kind of message than new or prospective customers, and the better you tailor your messages to fit what they're looking for, the higher your chances are of retaining and converting them. At the same time, when you segment your email lists, you avoid the mistake of sending too many unnecessary and irrelevant emails, which puts you at risk of getting marked as spam.

It's very rare that a cold lead is going to buy anything from you right away. You need to build their interest and trust over time and sending the kind of emails that will persuade them to come over to your site is the best marketing approach you could take. Cold leads are not going to be interested in a business that goes in for the kill right away, pushing and hard-selling their products right from the start. In fact, that's the quickest way to turn a cold lead even colder. A smart marketer would utilize the email list to build trust and generate interest over time.

As an example of what segmenting can do for your marketing, let's say that you own a pet store that specializes in selling products for dogs and cats. Now, if you sent out an email marketing newsletter that featured cat products to a dog owner, you're not going to make a lot of sales *unless* that dog owner happens to own cats too. But if you divide your email list into segments, in this case, one segment for dog owners and another for cat owners, you can send emails to cat owners featuring your best cat products and information on dog products to the dog owners. That's a much more effective way to ensure you're maximizing your sales potential. This same approach still works even if you're selling a service and not a physical product. Let's say you're a real estate agent. You've got many people on your email list, including a list of people you have already sold to in the past. If you send out an email with your current listing to your *entire* email list, the people who just purchased a home from you are going to delete that email (probably). If you segment your list into categories like leads, past customers, location, price range, and so on, you can send your new listing to past customers in a lower price range, asking them if they are thinking of upgrading. At the same time, you can send the same listing to past customers *in the same location and price range,* asking them if they might know of families who want to move into the neighborhood and encourage them to pass on the listing. By putting in the extra effort to customize your communication, you increase your chances of reaching your desired target audience. Could you imagine the possibilities?

Besides segmenting your list based on demographics, there are a few other options to go with. You could also choose to segment your email lists based on:

- **Lead Magnets-** Segment your customers based on the lead magnets that they opted into. If you have a lead magnet about SEO, you can create a segment consisting of people who opted into that lead magnet with a tag that says they're interested in SEO.

- **Using Opt-in Forms -** Opt-in forms may reduce the number of people who opt into your list, but you rest assured knowing that the ones who chose to opt-in are quality subscribers. Instead of just asking them for a name and email, you could take it a step further by asking for additional details like where they live and whether they currently own a website or not (still sticking to the same SEO example above).

- **Career -** Knowing the career background of those who have subscribed to your emails will make it much easier for you to specifically target certain products to those customers. For example, if you were selling educational equipment, you know the people who are going to be interested in your products would be teachers or students.

- **Product Views** - This list would encompass the customers that have already visited your site and delved into more details about the kind of products or services you have available. They would be the group that has already shown enough of an interest in the product or service to want to find out more about it. If you were offering coaching services on your site, they would be the users who are interested enough and possibly want to sign up for a program because they've already spent a certain amount of time concentrating on the service that is offered. A couple of persuasive, beautifully written targeted emails might be all the push that they need to take the next step.

- **The Almost-Buyers -** This group would be the customers who were probably already halfway into purchasing something off your site, and then at the last minute changed their mind before the final sale could be complete. Pay attention to this group, too, and find out what can be done to give them the push they need to make the final purchase. Think of including that material in your news email newsletter to them.

Why Email Lists Matter

Having an email list enables you to send out your content to multiple people simultaneously, which is a lot more effective than having to contact them one by one. This email list gives your business leverage because if you play your cards right, you could turn these customers into more than just email readers. You could turn them into paying customers. Most of the visitors who end up on your website for the first time are unlikely to make any purchases from you. When they leave, this results in a zero conversion rate. That's where email list comes in, by helping your business capture these very important emails so you can keep them in the loop, engage their interests and keep them coming back to your website for more. The more they keep returning to your site, the higher the possibility of them eventually making a purchase. When your readers read your emails, they want to feel that whatever you have put down in there is speaking to them directly, and not just a generic email blast with no specific group or target in mind. Every customer likes to feel exclusive and special, so make them feel that way and construct your emails like you would as if you were speaking to your readers face to face instead of over the internet. Make the reader of your email feel important like you have specifically tailored your product or service to meet their needs, make them feel special and they will keep coming back to your business for more.

Remember, if they've signed up for your email list, it means *they want to hear from you.* If you continue to provide good content, they'll continue to appreciate it.

Our emails have become a permanent fixture in our lives now. If you're like most people, you're probably checking your emails more than once a day too. With the introduction of smartphones, checking emails is now easier than ever since we can do it on the go. This means you're able to reach your customers at any time, no matter where they are. Here are some other reasons why email lists still matter (yes, they matter just as much as advertising on social media does):

- **Easy ROI Tracking -** Tracking ROI is easy, especially with email marketing software, which enables you to see which of your audiences is actually opening your emails. This option also brings in the highest ROI for your business because you don't need to put a significant amount of money into your emails in order to reach your audience.

- **More People Equals More Money -** It's simple business math. The more people you can send to your website, the more money you potentially stand to make. Emails still manage to stand their ground and, in some cases, outperform social media marketing, and there's a simple reason why. How many emails does one person get on average a day? 50? Probably not unless they're running a business themselves. Now, compare that to social media updates. How many Twitter updates do you think the average person gets? Or Instagram and Facebook updates. Unlike emails, content on social media refreshes every couple of minutes (sometimes seconds in the case of Twitter). Out of the two, which content do you think has a higher chance of being seen? *Emails.* Less competing for attention, and it's not likely to disappear from your view the next time you hit refresh on your page. Social media updates are going to drastically underperform compared to email lists because there's too much going on.

- **It's Personal and Power** - Landing right in your customer's inbox is a powerful thing. It's like going to where they live, ringing their front doorbell, and having a one-on-one conversation. That's how powerful of an approach email marketing can be. There is nothing that is going to limit your reach potential with your email list. You can reach out to as many people as you want without a ranking system the way social media has. You're not limited by keywords or SEO, and this makes email a very powerful communication tool. There's also that element of personal touch that goes into it since you get to customize your emails (even though you're sending out hundreds at the same time) and mention your customer by name in your email content.

- **It Builds Trust -** The best part about email marketing is that, if done right, it can be used to encourage greater customer loyalty. People read emails in privacy, on their own time. They don't have to feel rushed about it, and they can take their own sweet time reading the content they get because it's not going to vanish as soon as they hit the refresh button. By taking the time to read the content they get, they absorb the messages that you send, and if you're consistent with your branding and messaging, eventually, this is the style of communication they will come to expect from you. They'll learn to trust you and connect with you based on the type of content that you send them.

- **You Are In Control** - You are the only one who is in control of your email list (and your marketing team, if you're working with a team). Unlike social media marketing, your email lists are not going to be at risk of getting blocked or not being as effective as they should be when policies change. No, email lists are entirely within your control and it is not going to be influenced by anything else except your decisions and your actions.

- **There Could Be One Day Social Media Might Shut Down** - It may seem like a far-fetched notion, but it's not impossible. Technology, wonderful as it may be, is far from perfect and tech problems and downtime are not an uncommon occurrence. If one day you do encounter problems with your social media accounts for whatever reason, you lose contact with your followers, your audience, customers, and clients. If you don't have an email list as a backup plan, you risk losing it all. You always need a way to contact your customers and never rely on just one channel of communication. You never know when that channel might run into problems and you don't want to be left in the lurch.

- **Continuous Marketing** - The marketing never stops when you've got an email list. An email list encourages conversions when you're repeatedly directing customers to your website and marketing the latest offerings directly to their inbox. By personalizing your messages to fit your customers, you're telling them exactly what they want to hear and you're doing this repeatedly every week. Each time they see an email from you're they are reminded of your business.

- **It's Purposeful** - You could craft a brilliant ad copy but if the right people who are ready and willing to buy don't get to see the masterpiece you've written; your marketing efforts are still going to waste. Unless, of course, you have an email list that lets you disseminate your copywriting strategy in front of the right target audience. Targeted and purposeful, any marketing goal you have can materialize if you know the right way to reach your audience. That way just happens to be through their email, a medium they spend more time on than social media. You're not talking to a random individual or potential customer who just happened to stumble across your website. You're not sending out emails, shooting in the dark, hoping to get lucky. This time, you *know the audience* that you're sending out your emails to. Remember, your customers are signing up for your emails of their own volition. If they're interested in what you have to say, that's your opening to waltz in and make something happen.

- **Cost-Effective -** Emails are by far one of the most cost-effective marketing techniques at your disposal. Compared to the traditional methods of marketing, which relied on print, television, and radio back in the day, emails save your business cost in terms of having to print material, not to mention dealing with the high costs of advertising. Going digital and paperless eliminates that expense, which means greater cost-efficiency in the long run. The fact that they deliver a much higher return on investment (ROI) than conventional marketing methods do only makes them even more desirable than ever.

Chapter 2: Strategies to Build Your Niche List

Now that you know email marketing is certainly a useful, cost-effective medium for building relationships with your customers and keeping them informed about what's happening with your business lately, it's now time to turn your attention to the strategies needed to build your niche audience list. One of the most important and overlooked aspects of this process is the underestimated importance of knowing your audience.

Email marketing is heavily focused on copywriting. Where a lot of marketers start to run into problems is when they forget to keep their audience in mind when they're crafting their content. Marketers tend to forget that different styles of writing are required for the different types of audiences you may be speaking to. For example, the way you write a text to a friend would be very different from the way you would craft a text to your manager or supervisor at work. We know to adjust the way we approach these different situations based on our understanding of the audience's expectations and social context, and we often do this automatically when we write. However, audience awareness requires more careful consideration, and it can be easy to forget we're communicating with actual people sometimes when copywriting becomes part of your job.

The Importance of Knowing Your Ideal Audience

When it comes to email marketing strategies, most marketers are keen on focusing on what they can do to raise engagement, boost sales, and what they can do to grow the number of subscribers they have on their list. What they tend to forget about, however, is *what the audience wants.*

They're too focused on what they should be writing and the kind of content they should be sharing more of that they forget what the objectives of the audience are. They forget the reason *why* people decided to follow and subscribe to their newsletters in the first place and how to make the content they share relevant to their subscribers. But too often, marketers see their audiences and customers passive receivers of information, delivered by the marketer through the text (or in this context, emails). In reality, though, the meaning is not inherent to the text you create.

When reading what you've written, your customer and prospective customer forms an idea of what you're saying in their head, based on what's on the page, along with their own knowledge expectations and values. This leaves a lot of room for confusion and misunderstanding. So, it's your responsibility to speak to your audience in a way they will understand. The only way to do that, though, is to *know your audience.*

Email marketing is not just about sending another random email to your customers because *"it's your job"* or because you *"feel like you have to,"* hoping that a sale may or may not come out of it. No, email marketing has the potential to be so much more for your business, and it is time to start tapping into that potential for the benefit of your business. Each email that you send out must be purpose, vision, action, and trust for a successful outcome. You're not sending out emails anymore for the sake of doing so. This time, you're doing it with a mission in mind. That's why you created that email list segmentation in the beginning. So you have a clear idea of exactly who are you aiming to target through your email newsletter. If you've already got a good idea of the kind of demographic you're going after, a good strategy to employ would be to start customer profiling.

This will give you a better sense of what kind of content your target is after and the sort of content they might be persuaded by. Think of this stage as your due diligence. The more information and details you can gather to create your customer persona, the more definitive your marketing strategy will be.

What Is A Customer Persona?

Customer personas or buyer personas are simply a tool that companies can use to better understand their customer base. Most companies already have a general understanding of at least of who their customers are, often expressed in terms of demographics. Specifics like age, gender, household income, and so on contribute to the information you have to build a profile of who your customer is. A business also might have an understanding of psychographics and shopper behavior, so things like values and interests, as well as how much they buy when they shop, and so on. When you create a persona, you take all those cold facts and figures and use them to build a real living, breathing person. So for example, instead of saying that your customer is female, aged 35 to 45 with 2 kids, you take all that information and roll it up and say: *This is Joan. She's a working mom married for eight Yours and tries really hard to put a healthy meal in front of her family every night, but it can be challenging because she's busy taking her son to soccer practice and her daughter's riding lessons.*

By thinking of your customers *not* as a collection of facts and figures, but as a *real person*, it helps you craft marketing messages that better connect with that person. Persona development can also help inform media buying and media strategy decisions too. So using Joan as an example again, we know that she's a mom that is busy and on-the-go and doesn't have time to sit down and relax throughout the day. Therefore, marketing your content through social media channels is never going to be effective for her. One, because social media newsfeeds refresh and get updated far too frequently. Two, because she does not have time throughout the day to be consistently checking her social media every hour or so. Therefore, any marketing messages you're putting out there on social media are going to be lost in translation. However, we do know that Joan has her phone with her, even while she's on the move, which means she can check her email periodically throughout the way or whenever she's got a free moment and the email content isn't going anywhere unless she hit the delete button. Knowing all this makes your job as a marketer much easier in terms of knowing the type of content you should be creating once you know exactly the kind of customer persona you're dealing with.

One of the more interesting aspects of persona development are unexpected findings. It seems like every time you build personas for your customers, you come across some unexpected or underutilized aspects of that customer base. These new customers might not surpass your key customer base, but it's a great opportunity to expand your message to a wider range of people. Once you've developed a customer persona or profile you're satisfied with, you can begin working on building a niche email list and growing that list as quickly as possible.

What Is A Niche List?

In marketing, the term *niche market* refers to a group of people who are looking for specific products. For example, when a group of customers is interested in baby products, the ones who are specifically interested in *baby shoes* is your niche market. You could narrow that down even more and create another niche of those only looking for baby shoes for girls or those looking for baby shoes for boys. You simply take the broader audience and narrow it down based on very specific interests. Within one general market, there could be hundreds or maybe even thousands of other niche markets, depending on the industry you service. Sticking with this example, every day there could be hundreds of customers online around the world searching for baby shoes to buy, and that's where you come in and begin building a list of who these people are.

When you're building your email list, it's very important to *narrow your niche*. You need to select a group within the niche that you just targeted to find the highest probability. You're looking for the cream of the crop, the juiciest part of the niche. You may have heard of the *Pareto Principle* or the 80/20 Rule. The *Pareto Principle* was created by a guy named Pareto, who went and studied various types of systems, and he discovered that 80% of the results are always produced by 20% of the system. Within organizations, it turns out that 80% of the results are being produced by 20% of the people, and this is the way it is when we look at just about any complex system, including your email list. You want to target your marketing material to the 20% that is going to actually buy your products because this is going to give you the highest return on your investment.

Why does the 20% group matter so much? As it turns out, people want to feel like they're the only ones that your product was made for, like it was made just for them. Let's say you've got a splitting headache, and you walk into a drugstore looking for some kind of medication to fix or cure that headache. You're going down the aisle, and you're standing there looking at the Advil and the other Ibuprofen. Then you look up at the shelf above you, and you see a big blue jar that says *Medicine*. Which one are you going to buy? You're not going to buy the big blue jar that says medicine; you're going to buy the specific bottle that says *cures headaches*. We like to buy stuff that sounds like it was made just for our issue, and that example works in every context. That's why a woman who needs to lose 20 pounds in 90 days to fit into her wedding dress is going to buy an information product that's just about that before she's going to buy a general health product or a general weight loss product. Your customers, no matter what product or service you're selling, are going to think and act the same way when it comes to the solutions they're looking for.

Before you begin putting a list of emails together for your marketing campaign, always narrow your niche as soon as you find it. Once you've found it, *narrow again* and *keep narrowing* all the way until you run out of levels where you can narrow to. A lot of concern for many businesses and marketers is the niche that they've targeted has a lot of competition. So if your niche is one of these high emotional needs niches and your prospects are seeking solutions but there are many options, the way to solve the problem is to *narrow your niche*. This is a critical key. This is one of my secrets that you can use to create a lot of success.

Niche Building Strategy #1 - Developing Your Website or Blog

Successful marketing is a combination of having the right content and then making sure that content is seen by the right group of people using a combination of several techniques. To grow your niche email list, you need to have either a website or a blog of some sort where you can incorporate your list building software. A website or blog is going to be one of your business's most credible features. In the digital world, credibility is everything these days. Your website or blog is going to be the face of your business, the one that represents your presence online to your customers. No customer is going to trust a business without a website or blog they can refer to. Customers need details and as much information as possible for them to decide whether or not they can trust your business.

Without trust, your business will quickly crumble and fall behind, losing out to your competitors. Building trust is something that needs to be done right from the very beginning, especially new customers. You've got a limited window of opportunity to draw them into your fold, and this must be taken seriously.

Why is building trust so important? Because email subscribers are putting their trust in your business. To show that you value them and their belief in your business, you need to return the favor by letting them know that they can trust you in return. That is how you strengthen your relationship. That is how to retain them and keep them on as loyal customers. Since you can do that face to face with every single customer, your website or blog is going to act as the face of your business. Trust is even more crucial today because it is unfortunate that spammers have abused that trust and caused many people to become suspicious of email marketing. This makes the job of any business much harder, but not impossible.

Some people say content is king, which means the better your content, the easier it will be to get people visiting your site, and that would mean more money flowing in. The right content can go a long way to help you generate the most out of your website or blog. A winning website that is going to generate results must have the following elements:

- Brand-specific lead magnets that are located at the top of your website, so they are hard to miss.
- Prioritize content that adds value and quality rather than quantity.
- A call-to-action at the end of every piece of content you post on your website.
- Use pop-ups sparingly to avoid annoying your audience. A pop-up either at the start

or at the end as they are about to leave the website usually works best.

- If you have social proof of your past success, share it on your website so others can view it too.

- List the benefits of your products or services in bullet points for easy reading in the content that you post.

- Include appealing visuals that are attractive enough to get your customers to pause and slow down when they scroll through your website or blog to study the image.

- Promotes your social media platforms, which are also used to disseminate information about your business.

Niche Building Strategy #2 - Creating Landing Pages Perfectly

Your customers always want to see something of value, whether they're clicking on your emails or arriving on your website. If you want to grow your email list quickly, you need to create the perfect landing page for them to arrive at when they come to your website or blog. You only have a few crucial seconds to make a good first impression. How do you make an impact that lasts? To prove to your audience that yes! Your company is the right company for them? *With your landing page.* If you're serious about getting real results with your marketing campaign and watching your email list grow steadily every day, then this the one tip that you don't want to ignore.

You need to be able to grab your audience's attention and keep them interested enough to think, *"Yes, I want to subscribe to these email updates."* A landing page that is well-constructed is your best chance of achieving better ROIs, and whether they turn into paying customers or not is going to depend entirely on what they see when they land after that "click." A quick rule of thumb to remember when constructing your landing page is, the better your design and copy, the better the conversions you will see.

Your landing page needs to be as visually appealing as possible. The visual elements will go a long way towards generating some real results. We are, by nature, very visual creatures, and we want and are drawn towards anything that catches our eye. The human brain is also used to processing images much faster than texts, so be sure to use relevant, appealing, and enticing videos that speak to your audience and immediately draw them in. When thinking about what to put on your landing page, ask yourself if this is an element that is going to contribute to your overall marketing goal? If it isn't, maybe it's best to leave it out of the equation. You only want to include elements that are going to help build your trust and credibility as a brand in the mind of your audience. The fewer distractions you have on your landing page, the better the results you're going to get.

Niche Building Strategy #3 - Easy and Attractive Opt-in Forms

Opt-in forms on your website or blog are going to encourage your customers to subscribe to your updates. Opt-in forms in the right place at the right time can do wonders to boost your email list subscriptions. In Chapter 1, we talked about exit pop-ups. There is a free tool called *Hellobar.com* that helps you quickly and easily exit pop-ups. You might think that these pop-ups are annoying, but guess what? *They work.* Especially when you put them at the end, just before your customers are about to leave your page and they like what they've seen so far.

Is there anywhere else on your website you could include an opt-in email signup form? Yes, there is. Add the email signup forums at the top of your sidebar at the top of your page. Even better, add an email sign-up form on your "About" page too.

Keep your opt-in forms easy, simple, and attractive. Eliminate clutter from your design (and this includes your website or blog design) because is the number one conversion killer on web designs. In 2000, Sheena Iyengar and Mark Lepper conducted the *Jam Experiment*, which proved that when people were confronted with too many different decisions to make and too many options to choose from, they tend to walk away way from that decision process and choose *no option at all*. When you have a cluttered website, blog, and there are too many things for people to click on, people often decide to click on *nothing and leave your site*, never to return. The same goes for email signup forms. If there's too much clutter on your website, people are not going to sign up for your mailing list, because they're going to be overwhelmed with too many options.

To encourage people to sign up for your content, it was mentioned in Chapter 1 that you need to offer some kind of incentive. Something of value that is going to make it worth their while. More importantly, you need to *deliver on what you promised,* or they are not going to be subscribed for long. If you offered them access to a free eBook or a discount on a limited edition product that other customers might not have access to, if they're not subscribed, then you must be able to deliver on that promise. This goes back to the trust factor. Remember, your customers can't see you face to face. To them, all they have to connect with you on is your website or blog. When they give you their email address, they want to know exactly what they are signing up for, and it is your responsibility to make that clear. When they read your emails, they should never feel a sense of confusion about why they're receiving that email.

Niche Building Strategy #4 - Niche-Specific Lead Magnets

With the email list that you have, you want to create and send lead magnets that are going to prepare your customers and prospects for the sale. If you're in an industry where there are hundreds or thousands of lead magnets, look at them and think about ways where you can outdo your competitors. If your competitors are offering a lead magnet that says *10 Ways to Boost Your ROI,* you offer then *15 Ways to Boost Your ROI.* Outdo your competitors with just sheer numbers and share content volumes. The idea of a lead magnet is that *only your lead wants to read it,* no one else. If the information doesn't relate to them, they're not going to be interested. Your lead magnet needs to be short and simple, but ultra-specific. If it's vague, your customers are quickly going to lose interest and leave.

Create an irresistible lead magnet is to help save people time. Once you've crafted your perfect content, go the extra mile by giving them swipe files, templates, or things that they can use over and over again. This makes it feel like an actual deliverable, and when your customers are pleased with what they're getting, they're more likely to opt-in and convert to paying customers. Instead of offering them a *7-Day Email Course to Grow Their Email List, give* them the 7-Day course *plus* files and templates they can use repeatedly in their business. This is where narrowing your niche market is going to really come in handy. When you niche down your market, it's going to be easier to be as specific as possible with the information you deliver. Especially with new customers, where you want to offer some degree of personalization and highlight exactly why they should sign up for your email list. Your first email to your new subscribers should be something that outlines your promise and tells them exactly how you plan to deliver content or solutions that will make it worth their while and niche-specific lead magnets are great for accomplishing that goal.

Niche Building Strategy #5 - Content Upgrades

Content upgrade takes place when someone is reading your blog post. When they want or need more information related to that blog post, you can offer it to them using the content upgrade strategy. Let's say you wrote a blog post on *10 Ways to Scale Your Business*. The content upgrade you would offer would be a downloadable cheat sheet on the different techniques your readers can use to scale their business. Don't worry, you don't have to have any design or technical skills since you can easily create a cheat sheet and downloadable content with *Hellobar.com* too. Strategically place the content upgrade within the first few paragraphs of your blog post. Every time your readers click through your content upgrade, you get to include an email opt-in again, ask them for their email addresses so you can email the content directly to them and guess what? You just collected another email for your list.

Niche Building Strategy #6 - Long-Term Content Strategy

Great content establishes the right kind of relationships with your customers and prospects and enhances their perception of your brand. To keep your niche market loyal subscribers of your email marketing campaigns, you need a strategy for your content that aligns with your overall marketing strategy. This ensures that all those hours you invested in creating your content gets delivered in the most effective manner. Set up a schedule for how frequently you're going to be sending out your emails. You need to find the right balance, so you don't run the risk of spamming your audience's inbox. At the same time, you don't want to be too inconsistent with your emails because your readers will then quickly lose interest if your correspondence is few and far between.

Develop and determine the types of content that should be delivered to your readers. Once you've identified your audience personas or profiles, start to create a content calendar and the days you plan to send out your content. For best results, you want to develop a 30 to 90-days' worth of content to give you a clear overview of how well your content is aligned with your marketing goals.

Niche Building Strategy #7 - Utilize the A/B Testing Method

A/B testing is the process of testing two web elements to find out which performs better. Using A/B Testing allows you to test on two pieces of content and you can also test both large and small elements in your marketing. You can test something as minor as the color used for a Call-To-Action (CTA) to something significant such as a redesigned website page. When conducting A/B tests, you need to remember when adding more differences between two pieces of content is that you are only allowed to attribute the results to each piece of content that you are testing as a whole and not on singular or individual differences. For example, if you are testing two versions of one landing page against each other, and you have made changes to the CTA copy, the form length, the images as well as the heading on one of the landing pages, then you cannot attribute that landing page's success to the form itself. You have to attribute the success of it to all four elements that you have changed.

To run an effective A/B testing, you have to first identify the goal or result that you want from the testing. Referring to the colors of the buttons, do you want to measure how each CTA color affects the user's response to click on it? This method is among the most straightforward tests that you can conduct. There's no limit to the number of experiments you can run, and a A/B testing is not limited to banners. It can be conducted either through your email subject lines, landing pages, call to action buttons or logos.

Niche Building Strategy #8 - Use the Right Welcome Message

Engaging subscribers is a full-time commitment and what better way to do that than with a welcome email. These are emails that are triggered after each successful sign up on your mailing list. Think of them as welcome messages or reminders to your new faithful followers. They get the highest engagement rates from any kind of email, but you have to invest in writing the best welcome emails to get your subscribers to stay. Start with a greeting. Since you've asked for your subscribers' name when you registered for your email list, use it to your advantage. Welcome emails don't have to be bombarded with content immediately. A simple greeting will do. Adding personalization will go a long way, and emails with more personalized subject lines and headers are more likely to be opened.

Instead of saying, *"Hi reader,"* go with *"Hi, __(insert name___)."* This will make the email responses more personable. When setting up signup forms, remember to have separate fields for first names and last names so you can easily set up your email marketing software to change your content. At the same time, you can enable email replies to an email source, so people can get in touch with and email you for feedback. Depending on the email marketing provider you're using, you can look in their settings to find out the code is you need to put in to create this automated field that will enter the reader's name. Set up a call to action, too, because these welcome emails should lead users to take a preferred action. Use your welcome emails to push your users to do something aside from waiting for your next batch of emails. You can start by recommending your best content from different social media platforms or visit your blog for your previous content. Or, better yet, make a list of all the recommended content that they'll love based on the info you gathered from your signup sheet.

Be creative and pushing for your objective. If you want to sell a product or service, start promoting them subtly in your welcome emails. If you want to generate more interest in your courses, make a small introduction towards them. Setting up a call to action can make a difference between active subscribers and someone who just lets the emails you sent pile up in their inbox. Keep your tone light, friendly, and humorous where possible. Here's an example of a simple welcome email:

3 Easy Ways to Start Building Your Email List

Hi Sally!

Welcome! We're excited for you to be part of our team. As you're getting up to speed with our services, here are 3 easy ways you can begin building your email list with our quick and easy method:

1. *Go to our website and sign up for an account (if you don't have one already)*
2. *Download our available templates that help you craft the perfect welcome email (we've got plenty of options to choose from!)*
3. *Track your progress and stay on top of your to-do lists with our easy to use organization system.*

Look out for our next email on how to build relationships with your customers once you've got them to subscribe. Meanwhile, be sure to follow our social media channels below for even more exciting updates.

Keep it short; keep it simple. Make your welcome emails very special by giving up freebies. These are excellent for keeping your users happy through free content or discounts on their first initial purchase at the same time use this opportunity to tease your new subscribers with what they can get out of this subscription. It improves email deliverability and avoids it from being plunged into the depths of spam. Don't forget to remind them to subscribe to your social media platforms too.

Chapter 3: Email Subject Lines They Want to Click

The email subject line is going to be the very first thing your readers and customers see in their inbox. You want an email subject line that gets them clicking because that very first sentence and those few words that they see will determine if they're going to click your email open or send it right to the Deleted Items folder without ever reading all that hard work you put into crafting your content. 35% of email recipients decide whether or not to open an email based on what they see in the subject line.

Defining the Purpose of Your Email

Your emails are an opportunity for your business to become a great storyteller. Everyone loves a good story, and the more compelling your story is, the greater the reaction you stand to get. Your emails, especially the subject lines, should be more than just stringing grammatically free sentences together and delivering your message in a dry, bland manner. The only outcome that is going to achieve is that you'll lose the interest of your audience faster than you can hold onto that. With your email subject lines, you want to approach it the same way you would with the business plan you wrote when you were first starting out. In that business plan, you had a mission and a vision. When you were establishing your business plan in the beginning, a vision and mission was something you needed to give careful thought to before you set up your business. These set the foundation upon which your business is built.

A mission defines the reason why you are in the business that you are in right now, why you choose to go down this path, why you chose this industry. A vision then helps you define the kind of reputation you want your business to be associated with and where you see yourself in the future. *What kind of impression do you want to leave? What do you want to be remembered for?* That's now the same approach you need to take when you're crafting your emails and the subject lines. Becoming a great storyteller is done through great copywriting.

Copywriting, once again, is the secret weapon in your arsenal that has the power to make a vast difference. It can take a bland campaign from just mediocre to a campaign that leaves your customers wanting and longing for more. Copywriting is a very big part of your email marketing because this is where you begin creating a vision for your audience through your emails using only your words. This is the only opportunity that you get to create a vision that makes your readers believe enough in your brand to want them to take action. This action is what you've already pre-determined through the purpose of your emails. Good copywriting is a powerful tactic, and it can make all the difference in the world when you're attempting to create an equally powerful vision in the minds of your readers. Think about the vision that you want to cement in the minds of your readers when they open up your email and begin scrolling through your content. Do they have an issue or a problem that they need to solve, and only your business can do it for them? Some other questions your email should answer include:

- *What results are they hoping to see by using your products or services, and can you live up to their expectations?*
- *What benefit do they stand to gain by buying from you, and will your products leave them satisfied enough that they want to be returning customers?*
- *How do you create this desire within them to want to buy from your business and not your competitors?*

The Power of A Well-Written Subject Line

While the purpose of these emails may differ depending on your business, the industry you're in and the goals that you need to meet, there is one primary purpose that is shared across all businesses: *Email marketing campaigns are designed to drive sales*. Your readers think that they are in control of their actions. In reality, *it's you that directs them towards the course of action which you want them to take* without them even realizing it. Defining the purpose of your email subject line is so vital because without a purpose, you cannot direct their actions and you lose control. All the effort you would have put into your marketing tactics are not going to come to fruition, because you've missed out on this very critical point. The main purpose of your email subject line is to drive sales at the end of the day. As you're thinking about the kind of subject line you would want to write, consider the following questions and what you would like them to do:

- *Sign up for exclusive membership?*
- *Click your sales page?*
- *Join an affiliate program?*
- *Take advantage of the limited offer*
- *Download your free templates or eBook?*
- *Subscribe to your social media channels?*
- *Sign up for your webinar?*

There always needs to be a specific purpose in mind of an action you want them to take. After all, you are running these email campaigns for a reason. The true purpose of your email marketing is going to depend on what your marketing goals are. *How is the email that you're about to send related to your revenue model? How will it help turn cold traffic into first-time buyers? How will it help turn first-time buyers into recurring buyers? Can this email help turn your email subscribers into social media subscribers too?*

Every action should also align with your purpose and your marketing goals and this is why email marketing is not just to be dismissed as something that is ineffective. It is just as much a valuable tool as all your other marketing tactics, and it is capable of driving results when you clearly identify the purpose and the following action that is going to come out of it. Each email must be crafted with careful thought because, at the same time, you need to remember that you're trying to build a relationship with your audience too.

Writing A Subject Line That Knocks Their Socks Off

Your subject line is going to be the first thing your reader sees when they open their inbox. Perfecting your subject line is going to be the difference between whether your email gets trashed without a second thought, or whether your readers are intrigued enough to click it open and see what else is within the email. The worst-case scenario for a subject line would be having it reported or marked as spam.

To encourage your readers to open your emails, your subject line must give the impression that there is something in it for them. That they are going to benefit from what's contained in your email. People don't normally do things unless there's something in it for them, that's just the way people operate. Would you do something if you didn't believe there was something to be gained from it? Most likely not.

That sounds like a lot of pressure to be put on a subject line, which is often no more than just a few words or sentences, doesn't it? It is challenging, but not impossible. You need to start by first understanding and recognizing the importance of this subject line. Acknowledge that it is the hook, line, and sinker that is going to bring you the desired results you want, and therefore, a lot of careful thought must be put into it. It can't be something that is just randomly thrown together for the sake of having a subject line. Each word must serve a purpose because if you don't do a good enough job of capturing your reader's attention, you've already lost them before you even had a chance to get started.

Types of Email Subject Lines That Work

Catchy and attention-grabbing. That's how your email subject lines need to be written. The same way newspaper headlines are written because when you've only got 3 seconds to capture your reader's attention, you've got to make it count. They must be intrigued enough by your email headline to want to continue scrolling through the rest of your content. If you lose them during the first few paragraphs, you've lost them completely. The first paragraph should be an emotional hook, building on the curiosity of your readers and be interesting enough for them to want to engage in your content.

Then there's something else you need to consider. The fact that we're living in a world where things move so quickly, and attention spans sometimes last no more than 2-seconds before your audience has lost interest. Online users have an attention span that is quickly diminishing. If they're not interested enough within the first few seconds, they'll breeze past your content without so much as a second glance backward. For your marketing efforts, that only spells death, since you will have little to no hope of convincing them to purchase your products and services. No matter what, your email headlines are just as important as your subject line. The moment your readers click on that email, they should be immediately captivated by the first few paragraphs and sentences that they read.

Keep your email subject lines short and place relevant keywords in your subject line that your readers are going to recognize immediately. Filler words like *"Um, ah, okay, like, right, so"* should be avoided since every word in the email subject should add value and make your readers want to click on your emails rather than send them straight to the bin. Using relevant and specific keywords in your emails make it easier for your readers to locate your email later on if they do a quick search through their inbox, and anything that makes life easier for them is going to be favorable in their eyes. Every email that gets sent should be personalized to include the recipient's name, so it feels like you're speaking directly to them. A personal, one-on-one conversation between you and them, no one else. For your email headline to really get the job done right, it needs to convey the following characteristics:

- **Numbered Lists Subject Lines -** We're naturally drawn to lists, especially when there's a number that jumps right out at you. It's no coincidence that the content that gets shared the most on various social media platforms is the BuzzFeed-style numbered lists. So, why not take a page out of their playbook since it works so well? Examples of the kind of email subject lines you could craft are *10 Effective Strategies Your Business Cannot Afford to Miss, 5 Ways to Boost Your Social Media Presence, 3-Hours Mega-Sale Countdown, 15 Jaw-dropping Videos You Need to Watch.*

- **Curiosity-Sparking Subject Lines** - Email subject lines are a great way to peak curiosity among your subscribers and teasing what you're about to reveal is one way to go about it. You could also tease the content of your email with a simple statement, for example, *This Is How We Double Our Email-Open Rates, What*

Every Business Needs in 2020. When your readers' curiosity is sparked, the chances of them opening your email and reading its content are that much higher.

- **Quick Fix Subject Lines -** People want a quick fix and instant solution, and a subject line that addresses the relevant pain points is going to do the trick. Your subject line should offer a valid solution and targeted specifically to your buyer's persona or your specific email niche segment. Once you really understand who your buyer is and what it is they need *from you* to become a loyal customer, you'll know what their major pain points are. Want to sway them over to your side? Write subject lines that directly address those pain points from the very beginning and offer your readers what they are looking for: *A solution*. Even better if that solution is a quick-fix. This kind of subject line feeds into the need for wanting shortcuts. Offer them a solution and they won't be able to resist clicking your email open. *The Secret Sauce You Need to Ace Your Interview, Redo Your Kitchen On A Budget, Save Money with These Beauty Hacks, Travel Without Breaking Your Bank, 5-Minutes to Better Hair Right Now, Simple Tweaks for A Better Start to Your Day.*

- **Name Recognition Subject Lines -** A quick method to gain attention and build authority by proxy is to mention a name your audience already knows. Even better if they admire this name that you've dropped in your email. *Try Oprah's Productivity Hack to Get More Done, Mark Zuckerberg's 5-Best Success Tips, 6 Business Strategies Elon Musk Relies On for Success.* This tactic lets you capitalize on the influence of others, and within your email, you could give your own take on the subject and start building your own influence and authority among your readers.

- **Case-Study Subject Lines -** There are two reasons why people enjoy reading case studies. A case study is proof that a product or technique actually works like it said it was going to, and they usually offer a step-by-step process that others can emulate to achieve the same outcome. When you show them a case study and proof that a system or method works and you know that it is going to help your readers, mention it right away in the subject line. Examples of these subject lines could include *How I Got 200,000 Subscribers in 3-Months, How I Achieved Better Productivity In 1 Week.* Look at the data that you have on your current readers and customers and give some serious thought into what else you can do personalize your subject line according to what's relevant to them. When they look at your subject line, they should think, Ah! This is exactly what I was looking for, so they'll be more likely to click on your emails.

- **Exclusivity Subject Lines -** People love the feeling of being included, especially when they're made to feel special. Like they've got the inside scoop that no one else has, and this gives them the advantage. Since your email subject line is limited, your choice of words has to be as concise and succinct as possible. The right phrases in your subject lines can make your subscribers feel special, and the results will speak for itself when you see your sales numbers on the rise. Ultimately, your subject line should make it very clear to your readers about what your email is offering. This exclusivity can build a sense of belonging which will eventually lead to loyalty if they love the way that your business makes them feel. Examples of phrasing you could use include: *Insider Tips That Are Guaranteed to Work, You're Invited to An Exclusive Sneak Peek of What's Coming Up, Exclusive Offers Await Inside for Our Most Loyal Customers.*

- **Compelling Question Subject Line -** Asking the right question can draw your readers in, especially if it is relevant to them or addresses a specific problem again. Examples of such subject lines include: *Do You Know You Could Be Buying Instead of Renting? Is Your Website Making This Mistake?* People are naturally curious by nature, and if they are intrigued enough by a question, they won't be able to resist looking for an answer.

- **Fear of Missing Out (FOMO) Subject Lines -** The FOMO is real, and it has developed because of the modern world that we live in. We're constantly getting updates on social media by the minute, and it has cultivated a culture of addiction and FOMO. We live in a digital age where you can make instant connections and have immediate access to just about anything. We're afraid that if we don't check out notifications often enough, we might be missing out on something important. This psychological principle makes it nearly impossible for your readers to ignore your message. This acronym has now become a widespread phenomenon, and for a marketer, this is an opportunity to entice your subscribers to click on your emails by tapping into that innate need to belong to a group. Add an element of scarcity to your subject lines or words that signal a limited time, exclusive offer, and you'll have your readers fervently clicking your emails, so they don't miss out on what you're offering them. Examples of phrases you should include in your subject lines are *Don't Miss Out, One-time Offer, Exclusive Today Only, You're Missing Out On These Offers, Oops, Your Points Are About to Expire, Only ONE DAY to Download This Exclusive eBook.*

- **Funny and Humorous Subject Lines -** Besides that sense of urgency, the next best thing that appeals to a reader is humor. Clever humor or an insider's joke that only your audience will understand is a great way to warm up your readers and get them amused enough to want to read what the rest of your email says. Avoid making it too niche though, you want to keep the humor to something your audience will absolutely understand so the joke is not lost. Avoid movie reference or jargon that not everyone is going to understand unless you've got a very specific segment that you're speaking to. Steer clear of crass humor and jokes that are based on stereotypes too, since this could put you at risk of alienating your readers. Injecting humor into your emails is going to require creativity on your part, so if you're aiming for emails that are going to tickle their funny bone, give it some careful thought before you do. Groupon has a great example of a funny email subject line that went like this: *Deals That Make Us Proud (Unlike Our Nephew Steve)*. Open Table is another example of what a good sense of humor can do when they used the subject line *"Licking Your Phone Never Tasted So Good"* to get a laugh out of their readers.

- **Open-Ended Subject Lines** - People have a natural desire for closure. They want to get the full story and be satisfied with the ending, knowing they have the complete story, and tapping into that need is what makes open-ended email subject lines a winner. Their curiosity will get the better of them and they won't be able to resist clicking on your email so they can get the rest of the story. Ask a question, make a statement, or better yet, promise the reader something interesting if they were to read the rest of your content. Be careful not to over-promise or mislead your readers, though. Avoid that at all costs, even though you're trying your best to get their attention, this is not the way to do it. Misleading subject lines will only disappoint your readers, and they'll be unlikely to ever open your emails again when it arrives in their inbox.

- **Controversial Subject Lines** - These should be used sparingly since they might not work all the time. Controversial email subject lines include an element of shock or insult to get your readers to open your emails, but you need to be *VERY* careful with this approach as it could easily backfire on you. Examples of such subject lines are *"Why Your Marketing Sucks and What to Do About It, Your 5-Year Old Is Better At Social Media Than You Are."* Controversial subject lines are a gamble that could either pay off or fail miserably. Tread *VERY* carefully if you're going with this approach.

- **Vanity Subject Lines** - Who doesn't want to look better? Every single person out there cares about the way that they look on some level, even though they might say things like how it's the personality or character that matters more at the end of the day. We want to look good, and we could never consider stepping out of the house without looking presentable, acceptable, and decent at the very least. If you're in the business that sells products to improve and enhance looks and personal hygiene, for example, you could use this to your advantage with email subject lines that tap into the vanity aspect of our human nature. *Look Better With These 5 Beauty Hacks, 10 Tips to Help You Look Better In Photos,* are examples of the kind of emails that appeal to the side of your reader that wants to satisfy their need to look good.

- **Greed Subject Lines -** You don't have to be a greedy person by nature to want to jump in on a good deal. Discounts have a history of doing well because customers find it hard to pass up a great offer. Especially if that offer means massive savings for them. *Satisfy Your Wanderlust At A Great Price, Flash Sale 2-Hours Only.* Tap into your customer's need for savings and an unbeatable price and they'll be clicking your emails open faster than you can say the word "sale."

There's no hard and fast rule when it comes to crafting the perfect subject line. That's because things are always changing and improving. Techniques that worked well several years ago might not be as effective today. Even social media platforms and search engines are constantly tweaking their algorithms according to what is needed right now. Your subject line must work the same way. Stay up to date on tips and strategies for creating great subject lines, and always try to incorporate all the best practices to make your emails relevant to what your readers and customers' needs, and interests are. Ideally, you should aim to email your customers no more than once a day. Just sending them a quick email to touch base daily is enough to remind them about your business, without making them feel as though you're spamming their inbox with unnecessary fluff.

Email Subject Line Mistakes to Avoid No Matter What

Once you've put the finishing touches on that perfectly crafted email of yours, it's time to look out for any potential mistakes you might have made or overlooked before you hit the "Send" button. Scrutinize every detail because the email subject line is going to make or break the success of your marketing campaign. Therefore, it's vital to spend that extra time going over the details with a fine-toothed comb to make sure every email that gets sent is nothing short of perfect. Here are some of the most common email subject line mistakes that get made and what you should stay away from:

- **Using All Caps and Overdoing the Punctuation** – What if you received an email with a subject line that looks like this: *GET 50% OFF YOUR PURCHASE RIGHT NOW!!!! HURRY, DON'T*

DELAY!!!!. There's one of three things your customers are likely to do when they see this. They are either delete it, ignore it, or mark it as spam. Excessive capitalization and punctuation are off-putting to your subscribers and it will kill your open rates without question. Not to mention it makes it seem as though you're yelling at your readers, which can have a negative impact on your email performance. If you want your emails to succeed, stay away from the all-caps and going overboard with your punctuation.

- **Using Spam-Like Words** - Using certain trigger words that are spam-like can activate your recipient's spam filter, even if the content that you're sending is anything but spam. To avoid this, you want to stay away from certain trigger words like *$$$, 100% Free, Cash Off, Cheap, Weight Loss, Serious Cash,* for example. Even if your email makes it into their inbox, it can still give your email a spam-like feel since these emails give the impression that not a lot of thought has gone into producing it. That's why it is so important to choose the language of your subject line very carefully. The tricky bit with this mistake is that there is no set rule about these words. What works for one industry might not work well for another. You're probably going to have to try different variations of words to see what is going to work well for your campaigns.

- **It's Way Too Long** - The online world is a place where the short and the brief will thrive. The online audience wants content delivered and consumed quickly within a snap of a finger. If they have to spend too long processing or reading your content, they're going to lose interest and move on. Even a subject line that is way too long is going to be off-putting to them compared to a subject line with 5 words or less perhaps. Remember that your audience is going to be reading your emails while they are on-to-go most likely, and with only seconds to make an impression, your subject line cannot be too wordy or redundant. Long subject lines will look spammy and get lost in the clutter of the rest of the emails in your reader's inbox, even more so if your readers are using their mobile devices. Ideally, you want to keep your subject lines to nothing more than 50 characters, which is again why you should aim to cut out filler words since they are unnecessary. Only words that add value should be your priority.

- **Misleading Subject Lines -** This one is a cardinal sin. Don't make your email subjects misleading, because this will eventually put your readers off if they feel that they have been "cheated." Besides, not only is this tactic dishonest, but it will absolutely backfire and have the opposite effect of what you hoped for. There's no point in opening an email if that reader is not going to act on it beyond that. Even worse, misleading emails are going to make them feel angry or annoyed with your business and they'll probably unsubscribe as soon as it happens. No one likes to be deceived, especially when they receive an email that promises one thing but delivers another. Stay away from misleading subject lines unless you want to risk alienating your subscribers.

- **Not Running a Spell Check** - The content on your email is going to be out there for the world to see and you're going to want to make sure that what they are seeing is perfect spelling and grammar-wise at least. As a marketer, you should always be working and striving to improve the way you deliver the content before hitting the publish button. Read your emails several times over, check for any grammar or spelling errors, eye your content from a critical point of view and ask yourself how this post is going to add value to the person who is reading it. Spelling and grammar mistakes make a bad first impression and undermine your ability to establish trust and authority among your target audience. Always double-check and triple check your spelling and grammar. It's such a common mistake and one that could easily be avoided. In your rush and eagerness to get your emails out there, always spare the time to do a quick spelling and grammar check. Readers are not going to take you seriously if your emails contain mistakes that could easily have been prevented.

- **Not Hiring a Copywriter If You Need One** - The worst mistake any business could make is to cut corners to maximize profit. Sure, your business needs to make a profit to survive, but if you don't prioritize *quality* and invest in the areas you should be investing in, you're not going to be able to sustain yourself for long when you start losing customers. Not hiring the right copywriter for the job is one of those mistakes. Yes, it may seem like an easy enough thing to do to write and handle emails on your own, but copywriting is a skill that gets overlooked far too often and it has been a costly mistake too many marketing campaigns. Copywriting is necessary, and you might even say a vital element that is needed if you want to learn how to write emails that are capable of generating revenue. It is content of your email that is going to decide if your customers are going to read your content or send it to the trash without a second thought. The latter is something that happens far too often, yet it can be easily avoided, which just highlights the importance of good copywriting. Copywriting is the fundamental element needed for every email marketing. Without great copywriting, your emails are nothing more than just meaningless filler-emails to your readers. Another thing that is clogging up their inbox without adding any real value. Emails are an extension of your overall marketing and advertising campaign; it is an additional tool that is going to help you achieve the overall goals that you set out for your business in the beginning. Without great copywriting, it will be next to impossible to achieve that goal. If you need a copywriter, invest in one. Hiring the right person for the job is going to be money well spent.

A Short message from the Author:

Hey, are you enjoying the book? I'd love to hear your thoughts!

Many readers do not know how hard reviews are to come by, and how much they help an author.

I would be incredibly grateful if you could take just 60 seconds to write a brief review on Amazon, even if it's just a few sentences!

>> Scan the Barcode with your phone camera to drop a quick review;

Thank you for taking the time to share your thoughts!

Your review will genuinely make a difference for me and help gain exposure for my work.

Chapter 4: Getting Them Hooked from the Opening

Imagine if more customers opened your cold sales emails? That is every marketer's dream come true. What if you knew that turning cold leads into warm leads was a lot easier than you thought? Cold leads are the group of customers is probably the hardest one to convert. You're going to have to put in a lot of effort here to even generate a spark of interest among this group sometimes, and even then, it's not a guarantee. Cold lead customers usually have no inkling of who you are or what your business has to offer. When marketers focus on acquisition, they're focusing on this group of cold customers. It is difficult to convince them but not impossible. The key is to first warm up your audience with that very first email so that opens the door for you to begin building relationships and by nurturing your customers in this manner, you're nurturing the relationship and trying to get them to engage with your product or service.

Gradually, these cold leads become warmer as their interest in your product begins to increase. Once the lead has been warmed up, that's when you strike, offering them what you know will be the key to converting them into paying customers.

But First, What Is a Cold Lead?

Not all clicks are created equal. We have to understand the "temperature" of the customer, so to speak, as they come into our funnels. If somebody is landing on your website and decides to subscribe to your newsletters and your email opt-ins, what did they see? What is it that they liked enough to make them consider giving you their email address? How did they find your website? How did they hear about your products and services? Customers basically come in three different categories (or temperature groups), which are cold, warm, and hot. What you're aiming for with your email marketing campaigns is to push those cold and warm leads right into the hot temperature category because that's where the magic happens. That's when you see your sales numbers go through the roof, which is every marketer's dream outcome. Understanding the way these three groups operate is the answer to how to approach them with just the right emails and openers that will get them moving towards the "hot" category:

- **The Hot Leads** - These are your money makers. The customers that that already know you, they're aware of you, they've seen your work. They read your emails and they buy your products. With the hot leads, there already an established relationship. Since this group already knows you, the approach that works best with them is a personality-driven communication style. *Be authentic, be genuine, and be true to your brand.* You want to share stories, share your opinion and with every email that you send you,

you're directly or indirectly reminding them and answering the question of what it is your product or service can do for them.

- **The Warm Leads -** This group might not know you, or they just might be getting to know about you. They're coming to your channel or your product via Facebook Instagram or Twitter, and there's a good chance they could turn into a warm lead. So, there's a general awareness of your business among this group, but they don't know everything about you yet. In this case, the way to approach them would be to satisfy their desire.

- **The Cold Leads -** Anyone in marketing or business will tell you that the cold group is the hardest one to convert. They have no idea who you are, what you offer, or whether can trust you. What you want to do here with your emails is to provide clarity. You need to understand what the problem is, and then use the right email language to describe the problem in a way they can understand. Warming up a cold lead is not easy. It's a lot of hard work and not every cold lead is going to be as responsive as you hope they will be, despite your best efforts. It's important to persist despite the setbacks you face and keep pushing forward. Some cold leads are going to turn into warm leads, and for the ones that don't, that's okay.

Why A Good Opening Strategy Matters?

Without a strategy, you have no results. Despite the friendly nature that emails can take on compared to traditional forms of advertising, we're still not quite "there" yet where you can operate on a whim and email any kind of content you want, especially if you're a business. With the customers, it's a different story. An email marketing campaign needs to be dead on and hit the bullseye every single time, no matter what type of content you are putting out there online. You need to believe in your company's goals and vision, and that belief is going to be expressed in the strategy that you will now implement online. One of the cornerstones of an effective strategy is to

figure out what your audience is interested in talking to you about. That will give you an idea about what type of opening content you should be creating.

The reason why some email marketing campaigns fail and others succeed has little to do with tactics and everything to do with the strategy behind it. Common reasons attributed to a campaign's failure include poor email openers like the following:

- **The Lack of Original Content** - Avoid giving in to the temptation to post content for the sake of actively emailing your subscribers. The best strategy that you can employ for your campaign is to spend time collecting, refining, and curating your content to ensure that only the best gets shared with your readers. Every content that goes out to your readers should reflect everything that your business stands for. More importantly, it needs to be something that your target audience can relate to, and something that inspires them to want to take action. That is how you encourage and motivate them, and hopefully translate that into a boost in your sales numbers.

- **They Lack the Personal Touch** - It may be tempting to get right to the point because you're eager to achieve your campaign targets, but doing so at the risk of missing out on the personal touch aspect is another reason why marketing campaigns fail so miserably. Posts that sound too heavily sales pitched will make it seem like your business is trying too hard. Posting information that is inconsistent with the message you're trying to promote and too focused on the sale that it neglects to nurture the reader is going to be a big deal when your readers are not as convinced by your message as they should be.

- **Having No Subject Line At All -** If your subject line is empty. The message that you are sending to the reader about yourself is that you are lazy or thoughtless.

- **The "Hey" and "Hi" Opener -** Many spam emails are famous these subject lines and most of them are from senders that you don't want to have any relationship with. The "hey" and "hi" openers are bland, unoriginal, and do not tell the reader what you're trying to communicate so keep them out of your subject lines for good. They're generic, too clichéd, and there is zero originality and authenticity to it. Even worse if the opener starts with nothing more than just "hi."

- **The "Urgent" and "Important" Email** - *Please Read! Important! Urgent.* Your readers hate those kinds of subject lines. What is of high priority to you may not be that important to them at all. Could you imagine how frustrated your readers will be if your email turns out to be not that important at all? They'll be annoyed enough to mark you as spam; you can be sure of that. You don't want to be like the case of the boy who cried wolf one too many times. Your customers won't believe you the next time something is really urgent or important anymore.

- **Dear Sir/Madam Emails** - Again, these are boring, generic, clichéd, and completely unoriginal. You'll bore your readers and lose their interest even before they've opened your emails.

- **The Brand-Focused Openers** - If your opening sentences immediately jump to all about promoting your brand, your reader is going to hit the delete button faster than you can say *"Wait! There's more!."* They're not going to be interested because you're making your emails all about *you* instead of making it all about *them*. These emails will sound too forced and heavily sales-focused and instead of getting your readers interested, it's going to have the opposite effect.

- **Patronizing Openers** - *"You nearly did it. Don't worry; you'll get there eventually. Our tips will make you even better."* Your intention might have been to encourage, but the danger with this type of phrasing is that you come off sounding patronizing, rather than encouraging. Remember that the way something is written and the way it gets interpreted by the recipient are two very different things. A lot of miscommunication can take place because something was taken the wrong way, and when it's being read instead of spoken, it's very easy for wires to get crossed.

- **The "To Whom It May Concern Email"** - Way too formal for an email marketing campaign. It's cold, it's impersonal, and it completely lacks originality or creativity of any sort. This is not the way to start a winning email campaign. This is not a formal letter; it's an email. You need to have the first name of your reader in there, or there's only one place your emails are going to end up. In the spam folder.

- **Announcement Openers** - Using your first few lines to say, *"We would like to welcome you and introduce you to what our company is all about"* is another type of email opener you need to steer clear of. You don't need to waste those first few lines making a redundant announcement. Chances are if they subscribed to your email list already, they already know at least the basics, so you don't need to repeat those statements. Get right to the point.

- **Spelling and Grammar Mistakes** - Again, just like in Chapter 3, be sure to double and triple check your work. Emails with spelling and grammar errors are a big no-no. Take the time to proofread. You'll be glad you did.

Magnetic Words

Magnetic Words
Guidelines for Writing A Good Opener

To encourage your readers to keep reading your emails all the way to the end, your first few opening lines must win them over from the start. Your subject line was a build-up towards this moment. This is where you deliver on what you promised in your subject line. This is where you start painting a picture of your vision through your storytelling skills. Tell your readers how this vision is going to benefit them, what they can expect, and why it is going to enhance their lives. Your email openers should strive to maintain relevancy all throughout your email. To stay consistent with what you promised when they clicked on it. This is where you use your storytelling skills to convince them to take the desired action that you hoped for when you sent out this email in the first place. The subject line was there to help you get started; now it falls to you to take this pitch all the way to the finish line.

Copywriting skills are crucial at this stage because it is going to take masterfully crafted copies to sell your ideas using only words.

Another important tip to remember with your email openers is to resist the temptation to cram every piece of information that you have into that message. Put yourself in your reader's shoes. When you receive an email from a company, do you read through the entire thing word for word? Or skim through looking for important points that are highlighted? Most people would fall into the second category, which is why you must be brief and get to the point. Write down everything that you want your email message to say, and then figure out what the best way to summarize that into your first few opening lines. This is where copywriting skills come in handy once again, by summarizing all your key information so that your opening lines still pack a powerful punch. Remember that your readers have a limited amount of time to spare and they won't be encouraged to read through a lengthy email if they've got other things to do. Even more so if they're already bored by your opening sentences.

The first sentence of your opening line needs to be customized and very specific. Even if you're using a template, treat that template as a *guideline,* and *not as your exact opening line.* No, you still need to take the time (as much time as needed) to put careful thought into customizing your first few sentences because those sentences will be the deciding factor as to whether or not the rest of your email gets read. Here's an example of sentences that are going to get ignored:

Dear Amy,

We hope you're enjoying your Labor Day weekend! I know we are even though we might be taking a little time out to send you this quick email. Our team has a lot of exciting plans this weekend and we're off to have some fun after this!

Before that, we thought we'd send you this email to ask if you're interested in......

Now, if you were to receive an email like this, what would you do? Keep reading? Feel annoyed? Hit the delete button after that first paragraph? The sender of the email sent it with the intention of building a rapport, but truth be told, your readers are not going to be interested in what your weekend plans are. Why? Because they don't know you well enough to care about things like that. Clearly, they know you sent the email with a purpose, and it's better to get right to the point than waste those first few minutes of their time with idle chit-chat. After you've addressed them by name (which you always need to do), you need to get right to the point. Your emails need to be so relevant that your readers immediately know what you're talking about. The first opening lines should give them a compelling enough reason to keep scrolling down instead of opting out. Vague and, to be frank, pointless opening sentences like the example above is only going to get your email in the junk bin.

Keep in mind that the readers of your email are reading your content with their finger on the trigger of the delete button. You probably do the same thing yourself as you scroll through the flood of content in your emails, picking and choosing which ones you want to spend your time on. With precious seconds ticking away, you *cannot afford to waste any time* with overused, outdated, cheesy, and valueless opening lines that sound like this:

- *We hope you're doing great!*
- *In case you missed our last email*
- *Hope you had a great weekend*
- *Hope this email finds you well!*
- *You might be surprised to find out......*
- *Did you know?*
- *I trust that you're staying busy*
- *Hope you're having a good day*

- *We know you're really busy, but...*
- *Could you do us a quick favor?*

Stop, stop, stop. Those sentences are mostly for *you*. They make *you feel good,* not your reader. They make *you* feel like you're connecting while your reader is not interested in the least. These opening lines add no value and all they make you do is sound like every other marketer out there who has not fully grasped the importance of great copywriting and what a difference it can make. Most of the spam emails that end up in your trash all start out the same way. That's not the fate you want your emails to have when you send them out since it is not going to help you accomplish your business goals at all. Don't set yourself up for failure! You don't need those cheesy opening lines. It's time to stop sending generic, typical, and expected emails. Your readers are going to appreciate it when you take the time to send out a well-thought-out and carefully crafted email that gets your attention, holds your interest, and causes you to take action.

- **Use Language That Is Less "Sales-y" -** Put yourself in the shoes of your readers. Put yourself in the shoes of the person who is seeing all these emails come flooding into their inbox. Think about how language that is too much of a "hard sell" is going to look like from their perspective. Over-eagerness can easily backfire. Think about the most annoying salesperson you have ever met. The way they constantly badgered you and pushed you to make a decision about buying the products or services they were trying to sell. How did you feel when they overwhelmed you with information at the worst possible timing? That is what your customers are going to feel like if they're getting emails that sound like too much of a hard sell.

- **The Ego-Stroking Openers** - Make your reader feel special. Loved. Like they are the only customer your business cares about. Compliment them, congratulate them, use your email segmentation and niche targets to ask a question that is relevant to your target group's competence, background, or a problem they might have been dealing with for a long time. Emails need to be as personal as you can get without coming off as creepy. You're not talking to another sales number here; you're talking to a *person*. A person with feelings, thoughts, ideas, opinions. Empathy and compassion are going to go a long way if you can work this strategy into your opening phrases. Use the right tone when you're talking with them too. Be funny, be friendly, be compassionate, exciting, empathetic, compassionate. It all depends on the audience you're working with. Know your audience and approach them the same way you would approach a friend or someone you know well.

- **The Hidden Promise Openers-** The promise of forbidden, exclusive information is going to be an allure that is hard to resist. Curiosity will get the better of your readers, and they simply won't be able to resist reading through the rest of your email to feed into that curiosity. Be careful not to overuse this one, though, because your readers can see through your marketing tactic. *"I've got an idea about how to fix [address their problem], I came across this piece of content and I think you'll find it valuable, Our business just discovered one of the best solutions to solving [address their pain point], Our business can make a difference in your life and this is why."* Deep down, they know this is a ploy to get them to read your email, but if you craft your sentences well enough and keep feeding into their curiosity through your content, they'll be hooked.

- **The Ask a Question Openers -** People love to offer their opinion and they tend to engage a lot more when you ask them for their input instead of you telling them what you think. It's an opportunity to personally acknowledge and recognize a problem that your readers are facing. When a business shows that they care more about their customers' thoughts and feelings rather than just making another sale, they become more interested in *your business.* They listen more when *you show that you listen to them,* even if your email is not exactly asking for a response. Plus, opening with a question adds a little bit of mystery to your emails. Curiosity gets more clicks. Examples of what your opening questions could be are *"What's your priority right* *now? What do you think about [an event that happened]? What could you say if I told you I could make a difference to your business? Has XXX made your life easier?"*

- **The Surprise Opener** - Doing something unexpected is sometimes the best way to grab attention and keep it. Most of your readers receive dozens of emails daily and they usually all start out the same way. They more or less know what to expect when they open the email so when you do something that defies their expectations and turns the rules around, they'll sit up and take notice. Surprise them from the start and they'll be more likely to read through your entire email.

For the past few decades, emails have been the cornerstone of business communication, and over that time, it's developed a unique style and structure. Any business email you send should be clear, direct, and easy to read. The formality, tone, and structure of your writing, however, can vary depending on your company, your readers' subject matter, or other factors. No matter what you're writing, always maintain professionalism. Once you send out an email, you lose all control of it. The moment you hit *Send,* it's out there for the world to see. It can be copied, shared, even forwarded indefinitely. Your choice of words is crucial so as not to send the wrong message. Before you hit the send button, ask yourself this: *"Have I crafted an email that is going to have the impact I want? Or am I sending another email that is heading straight to the trash?"*

Be friendly and brief with your greeting and address them by name. Using their first name is preferable if you're more familiar with the recipient. Begin right away with your main point so it's easy to find and keep your writing concise and focused on your readers. If you need them to reply or respond in some way, include a call to action so they know what they need to do. If your email has a file attached, be sure to mention it in your email too so they don't miss it. As you reach the ending offer a quick farewell, such as thanks, or sincerely. Then give your name and contact information.

Avoid Getting Marked As "Spam"

The dreaded four-letter word no marketer wants their email to be associated with. If your emails are getting marked as spam by your readers or worse, they're getting sent straight to the spam folder without ever arriving in the intended inbox; it could be because some of these mistakes are being made:

- **Possible Spam IP Address** - Did you know that your IP address may have been used for spam? If it has, your target audience is probably not even seeing your emails since it's not even reaching their inbox. The best way to avoid this easy to fix a mistake is to use recommended and reputable email marketing service providers like MailChimp, Active Campaign Convert Kit, and Constant Contact, to name a few since these email marketing service providers are very vigilant about keeping their sending reputation intact.

- **Your Subscribers Have Forgotten That They Subscribed -** There's always a possibility that your subscribers don't remember you and are marking your emails as spam. People are on the internet so much, and frequenting so many websites, it's easy to forget what they're subscribed to. Every time this happens, though, it's a strike against you, and once that threshold is crossed, all future emails will land in the spam inbox. Don't worry, though, because you can easily avoid this with strong branding. Besides perfect email subject lines and winning opening lines, what you should do is include your logo, use consistent fonts and colors.

- **Your Open Rates Are Too Low** - Popular webmail providers will look at how many emails are open and how many are deleted without being opened as a factor in their spam filtering decisions. You need to keep open rates high by sending your emails at the right time, perfecting your subject lines segmenting your list and keeping your list fresh and interesting.

- **Old Lists and Low Mailbox Usage** - If your list is out of date and you're sending emails to those that don't exist, this is a red flag to spam filters. Keep your list up to date by sending a list cleaning campaign every now and then. Sure, you'll be reducing your subscriber count, but you'll be increasing your deliverability. Not including an unsubscribe link in your email is another red flag for spam filters. Making it easy for your email recipients to unsubscribe from your list can actually help your deliverability, so be sure to include a clear unsubscribe link in every email.

- **Spam Trigger Word and Clickbait** - A combination of both in one email is very bad news. Anytime you're inconsistent with your content, you put your email at risk of being viewed as clickbait and misleading, and even worse if you've got words that will trigger the spam filters.

- **You're Not Following Email Best Practices** - Email best practices are when a business includes a name in the "From" field that your subscribers are likely to remember. Don't change it too often to avoid confusion. Include your physical address since it's a requirement of spam regulations to include your physical address. If you work from home, a PO box will suffice (you don't have to share your home address). The other email best practice tips to keep in mind include using a maximum width of 600 to 800 pixels. Keep your image to text ratio low; you'll never want to send image-only emails, optimize your images for email by compressing them into a smaller file size. Keep your HTML code as simple as possible. If you're using a template from a reputable service provider, you should be fine. Don't use obscure fonts and stick to the basics of *Arial, Georgia* and *Times New Roman*. Make sure that your emails are readable and clickable on mobile devices, too, since most of them are probably going to get read from the phone instead of a laptop.

Find the Right Copywriter for Your Business

Some things are worth investing in and finding the right copywriter for your business is one of them. There is a letter written by *The Wall Street Journal's* copywriter, which has been described as the "best sales letter, which has ever been written." There are several reasons why this sales letter that was written was considered such a success, and among these reasons was because it managed to generate a profit of over $2 billion. This is yet another example of just how powerful great copywriting can be when a simple 2-page letter contains all the most brilliant copywriting tactics and strategies that successfully deliver the desired results. The letter wasn't overly complicated, tricky, or difficult to understand either. It may come as a surprise that the letter, in fact, began very simply by addressing the audience with a simple, opening line.

How did this simple introduction, followed by a few opening lines that set the scenario, managed to make such a powerful impact? It was an incredible success because it contained all the right, highly effective techniques that only a masterful copywriter can produce. After all, you don't get the distinction of being the best sales letter ever written for nothing. If you're searching for the right copywriter for your business, the following criteria will help narrow your options:

- **Industry Familiarity -** Your copywriter needs to be familiar with the industry that your business is in. That's how they get the job done right. By having a firm and thorough understanding of what your business and your industry needs, who the target audience is and what language is needed to boost your revenue. Looking for a copywriter who specializes in your niche market is going to be your best bet.

- **Your Business Needs -** What type of copy is your business lacking at the moment? What kind of copy is going to address your business goals? Deciding on what sort of copy your business is in need of right now will help you narrow down your copywriter search. Again, you want to try and source for someone who has a specialty in your industry and a knowledge about what your business is about.

- **Impressing Even You -** The best copywriter for your business is the one who is able to sell to you. When you read the copy that they have produced, how well can you picture the conversation taking place in your mind? Does it form a clear, distinct image? Does it tell you a story that you want to hear? Does it speak to you emotionally?

- **A Willing Listener** - A copywriter who is willing to listen and takes to heart what your needs are is the one who you should hire. Hiring the right fit for your team means the individual has to work well in a team. Not just with you, but with the rest of your staff who may be working towards a similar goal. They have to care about producing quality content according to what you need, and not be focused on producing any type of content just for the sake of doing so as long as it "gets the job done." You want someone with passion, dedication, and motivation to fit the bill.

Chapter 5: Copywriting Tips That Convert

A copywriter's job isn't easy. Not only does it require creative brainpower that helps you craft copies that knock the socks off your audience, but there's a lot of pressure that making sure every piece of content is valuable enough to generate the results that they were hired to do. Every marketer knows that good copywriting is the secret ingredient to success with any campaign that gets rolled out, including email campaigns. There are several strategies and different approaches that can be taken to ensure an email is as effective as it should be, but first, let's clear the air when it comes to the common misconceptions about what copywriting really is.

Debunking the Copywriting Misconceptions

Copywriting is not just about stringing several sentences together so that they make sense. It is part of a copywriter's job to try and persuade their readers, to educate them, to inform them and sometimes even to raise awareness about an issue or an event which may be taking place. These copies which are produced will end up on several mediums, including emails, depending on what your business needs are and where you need this content published. These publishing platforms could be anything from websites, press releases, newsletters, articles on blogs, brochures, television, advertisements, radio, and more. Yes, radio and television commercials are also written and created by copywriters. All those websites that you visit after a quick Google search. Every piece of content and information on those websites is created by copywriters too.

Copywriting and marketing are two very different strategies, although they both fall under the same umbrella of trying to enhance the sales of a business. Both these elements need to work together to create a winning campaign, *but* the job is not always done by the same person. A copywriter and a marketer could be two different people, or they could be one individual juggling two jobs if they are creatively talented in both, although the misconception is that both these job functions serve the same purpose. Here are some other common misconceptions that surround the term:

- **No, It's Not the Same As "Copyright"** - A copywriter is a "writer who writes a copy" (hence the name, copywriter). A copy is a written form of expression or communication, and it is written for the purpose of promoting either a business, a person, an idea or perhaps even an opinion. When you can't communicate with the audience face to face, you turn to writers to get the job done for you. They, in turn, will produce a well-written copy that addresses your needs. *Copyright,* on the other hand, is protection. It is the law that is in place that helps protect anyone who created original content. Original content in this instance includes musical content, literary content, artistic content and other intellectual material that an individual produces. Only the owner of the copyrighted material reserves the right to reproduce their work and to distribute copies of their work for sale. They also reserve the right to reproduce this content to lend on platforms that display their work to the public or even to lease out this content. Anyone who does not have permission to reproduce this content will be prosecuted under copyright law.

- **A Copywriter Is A Writer** - Another common myth since these are two distinctly different roles. Anyone can be a "writer" as long as you can string words and sentences together, but it takes a lot of effort and a very different kind of skill to be a copywriter who is good at their job. A copywriter has to take into account the audience and the platform for that they are writing for. They need to think about what they can do so readers actually read the emails that are being sent to them rather than just trash them right away. They need to think about how best to optimize their content for SEO. They have to think about how this content is going to come across on social media, whether what they've written is effective enough, whether they've missed out on any important detail. At times, they may even need to work with the graphics team or video editing team to ensure that their content runs smoothly and seamlessly with what the other departments are going to produce. It is not just about churning out grammatically accurate words and sentences. Anyone can be a writer, but it takes skill to become a great copywriter.

- **Copywriting Is an Easy Job** - Think copywriting is an easy job? Think again. Unless you've sat down and tried to craft the perfect copy yourself, it's hard for most people to understand that copywriting is no easy task. Writing content that is easy to understand *and* delivers the intended message to the masses may not sound like a difficult job, but make no mistake that it is. Why? Well, for one thing, great ideas are not just plucked out of thin air. Because copywriting involves a lot of research, planning, thought, and preparation which goes into the process before you can even begin sitting down and writing. Copywriters spend a lot of their time researching their material to ensure they have sufficient knowledge to begin even crafting the perfect content. And then there's the element of choosing and using the right words which must be accounted for to pack the desired punch that the message needs. Especially when writing for a business. You must have the right words that will trigger the right emotions to move a customer enough to want to buy from your business, and that's what makes a copywriter's job so hard.

- **A Marketer Can Also Do the Job of A Copywriter -** Another grave mistake that often gets made by businesses is the thinking that they "do not need copywriting." The more successful you want your business to be, the more important it is to find and hire the right kind of copywriters for your team. A copywriter is part of your marketing team, and every business knows that marketing is the lifeline that keeps your business alive and going. If you think this isn't true, try publishing content with poor or badly written copy and see what happens. Copywriters are the people who are responsible for your business staying alive and staying relevant to your audiences. Their work keeps customers coming back to you for more.

It Takes Skill to Seal the Deal

Copywriters are masters of the written word. It is their unique talent and flair for words that make them good at their job. Copywriters aren't just people who can produce well-structured sentences with excellent grammar. Oh no, they are so much more than that. The skill that copywriters possess is storytelling skills. A good copywriter works their magic sometimes without your readers even realizing it. They tell stories so good that it moves you and leaves an impression. The stories that they can tell about your business can produce feelings of excitement, happiness, anticipation, even sympathy if the cause that you are campaigning for is helping to raise funds. A good story can change the world, go viral, create a revolution; there's no end to the possibilities. But most important of all, a good story sticks in your mind and makes a memorable impression. Hiring a good copywriter for your business is how you level up your marketing game and multiply your revenue.

In your marketing team, your copywriters are just as important as SEO specialists because they write the content that gets picked up by the algorithms. Quality content is how you end up on the first page of Google search results. Quality content is how you make sure your emails don't trigger the spam red flags, and it is how you determine that your readers are going to devour your content instead of ignoring it. You need copywriters to help you get to that level. Copywriters are trained to focus on branding, conversions, and advertising, and they understand all the best writing techniques and practices too. They know how to build and maintain the personality of your brand through nothing more than the use of language. They understand that the selection of words being used will correlate to a certain degree of sophistication. One word is sometimes all it takes to differentiate between *"I need to read this!"* and *"This is a waste of my time, no thanks!."* They are the ones who understand that the tone of voice used should always be aligned with the brand identity that the business is trying to enforce.

Yes, great copywriting does indeed take skill. Here are the copywriting tips you need to keep in mind if you want to convert your readers:

- **Write Several Headlines** – Now, you're probably only going to use one headline in the copywriting but write lots and lots and lots of headlines because your headline is the most important element. It is the most important piece of copy in your entire ad. If it doesn't grab people's attention or get them interested, they're not going to read the rest of your copy, and you know this. Write lots of headlines until one really stands out to you and really grabs your interest, and that will be the one you use.

- **Think Like Your Reader** - Understand your reader and understand your audience. You really shouldn't sit down and write any copy unless you can instantly understand your reader. You want to be curious about them and know things, like what keeps them up at night? What are their problems? What do they really want that they're not getting? And, of course, how you can help them. Again, some basic research on your prospects is required and think like the people who are going to be reading your copy. Understand them deeply before you sit down and start writing. That way, you're going to ensure you hit all their hot buttons when you're writing.

- **Be Specific with Your Claims** - Too many times in copywriting, marketers make a big claim, but it's not very specific and, therefore, it isn't very believable. Basically, with any claim you make, you want to see if you can also be specific in your claim. You need to try and prove that those claims are true. An easy way to do that is to make your claim specific, like it was discussed in the previous chapters, back that up using numbers by using statistics. There's so much mistrust in the world, and there's so much advertising out there that your readers start to switch off, and they don't believe a lot of what they're reading. Which only highlights the need to back up your claims with proof. Examples of proof or credibility indicators might be testimonials, case studies, photos that demonstrate your product in action. They might be statistics, they might be proof about you and that you're an expert in your field, any achievements you can talk about and so on. But at the very basic level, you should be including case studies and testimonials, statistics, or anything that adds weight and adds proof to your claims.

Email Copywriting Best Practices

There are many types of copy to write for different clients, different formats, and different audiences. As you gain experience writing for different industries and niches, you will learn how to tailor your copy accordingly. Emails are typically much shorter than the other types of copy you would need to produce as part of your overall marketing campaign, so you want to focus on optimizing your emails as best you can in a way that packs a powerful punch for your readers. The following tips will help you develop a convincing copy that helps you and your clients reach their goals.

- **Never Write Without Doing Your Research** - Always do your research. Now there are two types of research that are essential to excellent copywriting. First, you must be informed on the subject that you're writing about and you must know who will be reading your copy. The first type of research is self-explanatory. If you're writing about the history of the music industry, you will have to make sure you know your facts are correct, and your stories are right. Readers and clients who later find out that your copy is inaccurate or wrong may not be able to trust the next piece that you write. There is so much information online today you'll need to be extra thorough and make sure that you're grabbing information from legitimate reputable sources. The second type of research is research about the audience who will be reading your copy. Every type of copy, whether it's a web page, email, or a brochure, it serves a very specific purpose. Do you want to inform, or do you want to persuade? What message Are you trying to send? Once you have established these goals, think about the readers who you want to see and receive the message, the following questions should guide your initial research: *What do the readers have in common? What does the average day look like for your readers? What values do they hold? Where will your readers view your copy? On mobile? Laptop? What issues or problems do they that you might have to research?*

- **Perfecting Your Preview Text -** Most of your client's emails are going to include a preview text, so you need to perfect that very first line they are going to see. It's the preview text that is going to make your readers pause their scrolling. It is the preview text that will tell your readers what's waiting for them if they clicked your email open. Keep it short, but focused and zoom in immediately on the purpose of the email. Keywords and phrases that immediately stand out to them are a good bet to go with. The skilled copywriter knows how important the preview text is and will spend the extra time carefully crafting that preview sentence. This is one aspect you simply cannot afford to neglect since this is where your reader is going to make the decision. To open or not to open, that is the question that will boil down to how good your preview text is.

- **Include Your Research In Your Copy** - Not many email marketers are going to think about doing this, so this is where you take your readers by surprise. Backup your copy with relevant facts quotes and sources, even if you have not built up a reputation of trust with an audience yet. Citing relevant information from reputable sources will help you get there, and your readers will come to see you as a reputable and trusted source. Tell your story through the statistics and experiences of others. Remember to credit your sources accordingly to the relevant legal and editorial guidelines.

- **Writing in Your Reader's Language -** If you have done some research on your readers, you will understand and should be able to write in their language. For example, the audience who is looking for landscaping services will not use the same terms as actual landscaping professionals. Readers with little to no knowledge of a subject will not be able to understand industry jargon. Knowing the language of your readers is important for your copy. If your readers don't know technical terms, they won't use those terms in search engines and therefore, they'll never come across your business if they don't read your emails. Find out how your readers describe their problems and phrase their questions, and what they're looking for what they think solutions to their problems.

- **Ask Questions -** Before you write down a single word, you should be asking yourself a lot of questions. In fact, the answers will help you while you're crafting your copy. What are your business goals and how does this email copy fit into your overall strategy to achieve those goals? What do you know about your readers who will be viewing this copy? What type of languages like the tone, style, and jargon will best represent your business or brand?

- **Write for The Style of Where The Copy Will Be Read** - The world of marketing, advertising, and writing has made huge shifts in the past couple of years. Businesses are investing more and more into SEO, content marketing, and other digital strategies like email and social media marketing. Content is being read across several mediums these days, like laptops, smartphones, and tablets, and you need to keep this in mind when you're preparing your copy. Keep your sentences short if emails are going to be read on smaller screens like smartphones. Most emails are either read on the phone or a laptop, so you need to keep your sentences much shorter than you would with let's say a blog post content for example.

- **Use Headings and Neat Organization** - If we paid full attention to every word that we read, especially online, we would get a lot less done. People want the information fast and they want to move on quickly. In fact, almost half of all readers are likely to skim content, so to accommodate this, format and organize your content so that readers will enjoy your content *and* get the information that they need. Always include important information at the top and use bold text sparingly only when you want to highlight key elements. Bullet point lists help to simplify the reading process. This makes the copy more appealing to readers users will be able to scan through your copy and find the information that they need very quickly.

- **Keep it Simple** - Paragraphs should be no more than one to three sentences in length for emails before you quickly move onto the next paragraph. Keeping the mobile phone context in mind, a good idea would be to double space between paragraphs so there is a clear and distinct separation. When you keep your language simple and concise and clear, you can get your message across faster. If your copy is compelling, convincing, clear, and concise, they will be more inclined to invest a little more time absorbing your content.

- **Use Imagery -** Using good imagery in written content is what helps engage audiences and pull them deeper into your story. In The Wall Street Journal's letter example talked about in Chapter 4, there was a sentence that read *"beautiful late spring afternoon"* and there's a reason the copywriter included this. It's because it helps to create an effective image in the reader's mind. Sort of like setting the stage while they told a story. Remember the storytelling skill which was talked about in the earlier chapters? This is why it is considered a valuable skill. Facts are great, but the way that you spin those facts into stories is the one that is going to sell your audience.

- **The Right Choice of Words -** Words are an incredibly powerful thing. The simple nuances between synonyms can make a difference and when you harness that language power, the message within your email copy is strengthened tenfold compared to if you didn't include these words at all. Some words like *"stuff, like, really, very, think, feel"* are considered weak crutch words that don't add any solid value to your copy. Sensory words are a fantastic option to consider including in your copy since they will raise your emails from bland to bravo. Sensory words are descriptive, often used to talk about sight, sound, smell, taste, and touch (quite literally the five senses that we use to navigate the world). Examples of such sensory words include *"deafening, towering, disheveled, itchy, ice-cold, bittersweet, pungent, flowery, delicious."* Combine this with the imagery point above and you'll be helping your reader visualize a crystal clear picture in their mind that will make your message so clear they're not going to forget it anytime soon.

- **Personalize It -** Avoid speaking to your readers like an impersonal, disinterested party. A good copywriting technique to remember is that you should always talk to your audience the way you would talk to a friend. If you were about to tell a story to a friend, how would you narrate it? Also, you want to write from a second person perspective because it feels more actionable, casual, and personable that way. This means using a lot of pronouns which include *"you, yours, and your"* for example. This gives the impression that your email copy is oriented towards your readers and not yourself, that it is all about them. Having a balance and use of second-person language will keep the focus of your email trained on your reader's, instead of focusing too heavily on your business. A subtle, yet effective technique because your customers want to feel like they matter to you, and that you value them as more than just a walking dollar sign.

- **Create A Unique Selling Point -** Also known as a USP for short. This is where you need to offer something to your readers that your competitors cannot. What is it about your products or services that make you special? Why would your readers benefit from you and not your competitor? What have you got to offer that your competitor hasn't thought about yet or cannot offer at this point?

- **Clarity Over Catchiness** - Your readers must be able to understand what you're trying to tell them, and that is why copywriters must craft content with clarity. Avoid making your audience feel like they are drowning in a sea of overwhelming information. Content should be clear, concise, and succinct. Never sacrifice clarity and meaning in favor of entertainment value or originality. Your readers might be entertained, but if the meaning of your message is lost in translation, you're not going to achieve the desired results or action you were hoping for either. Clarity first, catchiness second.

- **Align It All** - The best kind of copy is the kind where everything is aligned. It delivers on what you promised your readers in the subject line, it delivers on the promises you made in your opt-in and landing page when your readers first gave you their email address, it aligns with your business vision, your goals, and why you launched this marketing campaign to begin with. A good copy is one that reassures the reader of the email that they are indeed getting what they signed up for so there are no regrets on their part.

- **Zoom In On the Benefits -** There is a difference between benefits and features, and your email copy should focus on the former instead of the latter. A common mistake that many email marketers make is to dive into the features that their business is offering and forgetting about emphasizing why it is going to be beneficial for the reader. The benefits are the ones that highlight the importance and the value of your email to your reader. You may know your email's value, but your reader does not. Therefore, it becomes your job to convince them. When crafting your email body, remember it's all about the benefits.

There's always a goal behind your copy. You want readers to buy a product, trust your brand, or make a donation. Since you won't be standing behind your readers as they consume your copy, it's up to the reader to take the next steps and help you achieve your goals at the end of your copy. Therefore, you need to provide your readers with the next steps or list of relevant resources where should they go for more information. Who should they contact to make a purchase? What are other sources of content that can help them? This adds extra value to your copy and moves the reader along a process that is called *the buyer's journey*.

Biggest Copywriting Mistakes to Avoid

Every marketer or copywriter has been in this position. You've written what you think is a genius, brilliant piece of copy. You're feeling pleased with what you've written, but then you're disappointed to find your copy falls flat. You could have 10-years of copywriting experience and still not everything you write will turn to gold. You will miss the mark at times, but here's the good news. Your market is where you'll get your irrefutable feedback. Even better is that the results you get are going to be quantifiable. Your audience either loves what you've written, or they don't, and this is the perfect opportunity to grow your skills and learn along the way. Here's a little secret you might not realize: *Even some of the best copywriters in the world have written their fair share of bad copies. In fact, they've probably done it more than anyone.* But they've learned along the way and they became the best. So, if you want to increase your chances of writing copy that converts, here are the mistakes you need to stay away from:

- **You're Not Polarizing** - "*But my product or service can help anyone! I don't want to alienate anyone in my copy.*" If no one is buying your product, you're not moving forward either way. You need to polarize your audience. *Polarity means popularity.* If you try to help everyone you become a Jack of all trades but master of none. The greater the polarity you create, the higher the chance that your ideal target audience is going to be right there supporting you. The more they support you, the more trust you eventually build with them.

- **Focusing on *Features* Instead of Benefits** - Features and benefits was mentioned above, and yes, if you focus on the former rather than the latter, your copy is going to fall flat. A feature focuses on what your *product has*. When you're writing your sales copy, the features are going to be the factual and true statements that describe the details of your product, *but they are not* the aspects that will entice your customers and win them over enough to buy from you. Benefits focus on *why* your customer is buying your product. When writing about the benefits, you will describe the outcome in such a way that it will persuade your readers why they need this product in their life. An example of a feature is *"batteries included."* An example of a benefit is *"Ready to use."*

- **Not Thinking Mobile First** - Not optimizing your copy and websites for mobile-first will be the downfall of your marketing campaign. Always assume the readers are mainly going to be viewing your email with smaller screens and bigger thumbs that scroll quickly. Use shorter headlines and bigger fonts. Use succinct words like "tap" instead of "click. Make sure that your copy easy to read and flows on a small single column mobile device.

- **Your Words Are Too Fancy** – Your readers are scrolling quickly, and this means they are not going to recall what you said two seconds ago. The human brain, as great as it is, is lazy and loves cognitive fluency. The easier it is to understand something, the more likely you are to recall it and believe it. As the old saying goes: *If you can't explain it simply, you don't understand it well enough*. The goal of every sentence that you produce is to capture attention and generate enough interest for the reader to stay on your email. Unnecessary fluff and complex words will only break that connection you have with your reader.

- **Not Repeating Key Information –** Repeat so they don't forget. Once again, our brains are likely to forget a lot of information at surprising speeds if no repetition is involved. It may seem redundant, but repetition is necessary to get your point across, especially where the call to action is concerned. Keeping your copy short makes it easy to quickly repeat some of the highlights you want your readers to remember and this increases the likelihood that they're going to remember what you say even once they have clicked out of your email.

- **Not Including Your "Because" –** There must always be a reason why for everything that you do. This principle works the same way of everyone. If you didn't have a good reason to do something, would you do it? Your readers are the same. If you don't explain why your sale is for a limited time only, or why your refund policy works in such a way, your readers might not be convinced enough to react the way you want them to.

Chapter 6: Call-to-Actions That Win Them Over

Nothing pumps up the customer's adrenaline quite like a limited time offer. Or a special, one-time deal that's not to be missed. Creating that sense of urgency with a strong call to action encourages your audience to swipe up for more information or head directly to your website, which hopefully translates into a sale for your business.

What Is A Call to Action?

Better known as CTAs, every marketer who's been in the business for a while now will tell you that a strong CTA is a game-changer. A CTA is any method that explicitly prompts a person to take the desired action. Now, this can come in many forms, such as an image that says *Add To Cart* or text links that say *Click Her*e or even the spoken word which is what you'll find in a lot of YouTube videos when the speaker asks you to click the subscribe button or give the video a thumbs up. That's a call to action. Every page of their website needs to contain a call to action. Every email you send out needs to have a call to action. Every social media post and blog post needs to have one. Every video you upload for your business needs to have a call to action. *Every piece of content you produce must have a call to action* or it's not going to work.

If you want someone to sign up for your email newsletter, then there needs to be a sign-up button. If you have a blog, there should be related articles at the end of the blog post that people can click on to continue further. Or if they want your readers to subscribe to your social media sites or call you, then you need to have their telephone number there with *Call Us Now* or *Set Up An Appointment Now* and links to your social media sites. Whatever it is, there needs to be something to tell the person what to do next in order to engage with your content further or to take the next step in your sales funnel.

When dealing with calls to action, you need to make sure that these CTAs are explicit because you shouldn't assume that a person visiting your website knows what the next step is. You need to explicitly tell them what to do next and you should use action verbs that are related to the desired result. So, if you want someone to sign up for your email newsletter, don't use the word "submit" unless you want the person to be submissive. Instead, you should use words like, *send me my free report*, or *send me more tips*, things like that. The best way to get people to take action is to get them to sit up and pay attention. If your ad has got a call to action, put it right smack in the middle where it's going to be hard to miss. This is also great for capturing the attention of already interested readers who are engaged with your content. Video hosting company *Wistia* discovered that placing a call to actions in the middle of the videos resulted in a much higher conversion rate of 16.95% compared to call to actions, which were either at the start or at the end of videos. Call to actions at the start of videos only had a 3.15% conversion rate, while a call to actions placed at the end of videos was at 10.98%.

The same approach can be taken with any piece of marketing material that you produce, not just videos. It works for emails, for websites, social media platforms, blog posts, and any other content you produce *as long as your CTAs are obvious and hard to miss.* You will be surprised at how blind people can be when the thing that they're looking for is right there in front of them and they just don't see it. Your readers can miss a lot, even though something is right in front of them and even more so because they're scrolling through content quickly, especially email content. Businesses have the option of choosing from six different types of basic calls to action buttons:

- Apply now
- Click here
- Sign up now
- Download now
- Subscribe
- Get a quote

A call to action is a necessary part of your lead generation process, too, because it shows your user exactly what the next step they need to take should be. It leaves no question about the action that should be taken for results, and it is also the way that your business urges them towards a conversion. If they take the trouble to fill in the form, then they must be really interested in what your brand is offering. It won't take much more to convert them into paying customers from here. These are high-quality leads that you most certainly don't want to slip through your fingers.

CTAs Are Your Icing On The Cake

All the hard work you've done has led up to this moment. The hours you spent pouring over the details of your copy to make sure every detail is perfect. All you need now is for your readers to take that final step and you've crossed the finish line of the goal you set out to accomplish. The CTA is a very last, very vital ingredient of your marketing recipe. Without it, your efforts won't be as successful. Don't hold back on it and don't be afraid to repeat it. A successful marketing campaign will not exist without it. Your conversions, the ability to generate revenue and profit, and even to garner new business are all highly dependent upon having a powerful call to action that drives your audience to make a purchase. Unbounce's Michael Aagard, a business's CTA is like the "tipping point," the difference between a bounce and a conversion.

There are plenty of calls to action which a business could take. Whenever you want your audience to respond or take action in some way or another, your CTA should be there to get the job done. Some examples of CTAs include *Try It Now, Buy Now, Signup Now, Subscribe Now, Add to Cart*, or even forms designed to gather information. Social media widgets and share buttons could also be considered CTAs. Your readers your primary target market. When crafting a CTA, you need to craft it with them in mind. The copy can consist of something as simple as *Shop Now, Call Now, Book Now*, or something to that effect depending on what the content of your copy is about. The CTA is designed to ignite a response within them, and the copy of the CTA should do just that. You will know that your CTA is successful when you've managed to get your audience to take some action.

Crafting the Perfect CTA

Persuasive, creative, compelling are necessary ingredients that need to be added into the CTA mix. A CTA must entice your audience to take action. This is the only rule of thumb you need to remember when you think about your calls to action. You don't want them to be just scrolling past your copy, looking at it, reading it, but then doing nothing about it. You want them to buy or sign up with your brand. You want to turn them from a mere observer into a loyal customer. That's what you're aiming for and those are all the elements that need to come through when you're crafting out your CTA.

Where you place your CTA is just as important as what it says. Where is it going to appear on the email copy? What is it going to say? Tim Ash, CEO of SiteTuners, says an effective CTA needs two key elements. The first is that your visitors must be able to immediately notice your CTA without any effort at all. It basically needs to be hard to miss.

The second element which must occur is that just by looking at your CTA, your audience immediately knows what to do without any further instruction. Other key aspects involved in contributing to the success of a CTA:

- **Well-Designed and Easy to Recognize** - A striking CTA in your marketing material is one that going to be hard to miss. An effective CTA is one that is instantly recognizable. Your CTA should also be well-defined. Your readers should be able to open your email, go to your blog, your website, and your social media sites, and immediately know which button represents your CTA. It doesn't have to be too complicated or overly fancy. It's more important that it is recognizable than anything else. When including it into your email copy, emphasize it. Type it out in bold or capital letters so it stands out. If you're including it in a visual ad copy, highlight the CTA in bigger, bolder, or contrasting colors. Anything that is going to make it crystal clear that this is, in fact, the CTA audiences should be paying attention to.

- **Mind Your Language** - Even with something as simple as a two-word CTA, the language you use matters, just like every other sentence in your email copy. The 6th edition of the Holt Handbook, when the verb contained within a sentence is one that is active, the subject (audience/website visitor) will act or do something. When creating your CTA, be sure to only use active verbs within the copy. The words that you choose to use should be action-oriented and as strong as possible. The keyword that you want to focus on is action, and when you craft your CTA, you need to ask yourself if the words you have chosen are strong enough to spur someone to action. Some examples of action words include buy, order, discover, get, and subscribe. The words that you choose to use must communicate to your readers that they will be getting something of value. That their action is going to result in something worthwhile at the end.

- **Perfectly Placed** - Repeat this to yourself as many times as needed so you never overlook this aspect. A perfectly placed CTA equals more conversion is likely to occur. Your CTA should be in the middle and at the bottom of your email, so your audience is immediately able to spot it. Your CTA should not be so overpowering that it competes with the rest of the content, though. What works best is if you work your CTA into your copy so that it blends seamlessly and doesn't look too out of place.

- **Visually Appealing** - If you can work some visuals into your emails, you should do exactly that where your CTAs are concerned. Striking visuals that are sure to capture your audience's attention means they're not going to miss your CTA when it is the most striking thing in your copy. If you are planning to include visuals, design CTAs that are going to draw your readers in. Think about the typeface, the colors and the images that you're going to use, and how you can combine these elements together to create an ad so striking that it is going to stop your readers scrolling through your email just so they can take a second look at your call to action. Your CTA should be so clear that it leaves little room for doubt about what action the reader needs to take next. When your reader responds to your CTA, they should already know what to expect.

Magnetic Words

The Success of Your Campaign Depends On It

When you have a goal, it makes it easier to incorporate an effective call to action within that copy. Without that, your readers are unsure about what they should do with the information you have just presented them with. Your CTA needs to be everywhere, and this cannot be stressed enough. It has to be in every piece of copy you produce (whether it is emails, visuals, or videos), and it absolutely without a doubt must be on your website too. For marketers and advertisers, a CTA is their golden opportunity to motivate their readers towards taking some real steps to becoming paying customers. A CTA has become such a marketing copy staple that going without it is going to spell disaster for your ad campaign. If there is a fine line between a lead and conversion, that fine line is the CTA. Your CTA is the finishing touch to a perfectly well-executed ad campaign. Whether it's subtle or blunt, your CTA must be an

181

essential part of any marketing campaign that you're running if you want to finish that campaign on a high note.

Whether you're looking to create a sense of urgency with your CTA, or just using it as a boost to prompt your audience to take the next step, your CTA must be present regardless. With the right CTA in place, the results will be sure to follow eventually. A CTA is designed to boost the success of your campaign. You want your readers to be talking about your brand. Therefore, your CTA is the piece of the puzzle that you don't want to miss. You need an inspirational hook to reel in your audience. CTAs are a catalyst for your sales funnel. That crucial moment when a buyer is trying to decide if they should take the final step and make a purchase is when your CTA is going to make all the difference. The CTAs will be responsible for subtly prompting and remind your audience to take action, and a well-placed CTA will be the one that drives sales.

Great CTAs will highlight what benefits the audience stands to gain if they take some action now. For example, *"Sign up now for 15% off your first purchase!"* It is a very motivating CTA indeed. An effective CTA is one that creates great experiences for your audience. The CTA will do all the work for them. They don't have to guess, wonder, or question what they should do next. All the answers they seek are located within that simple CTA, and that can be all the motivation they need to decide to make a sale. Your readers actually *want* to see a CTA and they will be turned off whenever there is no CTA at the end of the button. That's how much they have come to expect seeing it as part of the ad. They have even come to depend on CTAs to show them what the next steps should be taken. Without even realizing it, readers look out for CTAs subconsciously for their next instructions. This is why if your marketing campaigns are missing this very vital tool, you're not going to get very far. CTAs are predictable, but this is the kind of predictability that you want for your business. Strong CTAs have become a staple and if your emails do not have a CTA, you're missing out on a big conversion opportunity.

Call to Action Mistakes That Are Killing Your Conversion Potential

No marketer wants to experience that dreaded moment when they realize their campaigns are not converting. Your copy is written perfectly, and you've triple checked to make sure there were no mistakes when you sent out that email this morning. So why isn't your campaign performing the way that you hoped it would? Probably because you're committing these CTA mistakes and didn't even know it:

- **Like A Game of Where's Waldo -** Is your CTA too difficult to find? That could be one of the reasons why you're not getting the results you want. Keep in mind that most of your readers are probably skimming and scanning your content so they can get through it as fast as possible. Some don't have the luxury of taking their own sweet time when they read and if your CTA is too hard to find or not obvious enough, they're not going to bother looking for it at all.

- **Your Options Are Overwhelming -** To you, it might seem like a good idea to present your reader with as many options as possible, so they're spoilt for choice. With so much to choose from, there's no reason why they should go looking elsewhere for an answer when you've given them everything they need right here. To some of your readers, having *too many options* is not a pleasant scenario at all. With so much to choose from, they don't know where to begin and how to decide if they're making the *right* choice for them. If that seems overwhelming, that's because it is. When you're faced with a decision you realize could potentially change your life forever, there's definitely some pressure that comes with that realization. Some people are so afraid of making decisions that they suffer from what's known as decision paralysis. That's understandable, especially when faced with important decisions. You want to do everything you can to make sure you get it right. As stressful as choices can be, your readers still need to make them since they don't want to feel like they have no choice in the matter at all. The trick is to give them specific, selected options and in the process, help them narrow down their choice through the story you tell in your copy and call to action.

- **Too Long and Too Tricky** - Simplicity is the key to winning with your CTAs. Your time to play around with creativity and extra information was in your copy. Your CTA is where you get right to the point. If it's too long, too tricky, and involves far too many complicated steps, your readers are going to throw their hands up and say they've had enough.

- **Not Using Colors -** If your CTA blends in with the rest of your content, it's going to be easy to overlook it. A CTA that is hard to miss is one that pops and stands out among a sea of black and white print. A common mistake that gets made by a lot of marketers, especially where email is concerned, is to keep the copy all one color and save the flashy colors for their other advertising material. Oh no, your email is also a part of your marketing campaign and if anything, *this* is where your CTA really needs some color to attract attention. If your readers don't notice much about your email, at least be sure that they are noticing your CTA.

- **Having Several CTAs In One Copy -** Pick one CTA and don't move away from it. Having multiple CTAs scattered throughout your email is going to be confusing and off-putting. You need to make it as easy as it can get for your readers, holding their hand every step of the way so very little effort and thinking is required on their part. The minute you try to complicate a simple process is the minute you lose them. Pick one CTA and make that your CTA throughout your email. Be consistent.

- **Not A/B Testing Your CTAs -** You always need to test it to see what's working and what isn't. It's like an experiment; you need to try several different combinations before you come up with the winning

Magnetic Words

formula. test try a couple of different CTAs, see what works better. Maybe run one for a month and see how it performs, then run another one for a month and see how that performs and then compare the data and then use what's working. Think of a couple of variations and A/B test that so you ultimately end up with the best product at the end of the day. The A/B testing system is a more reliable approach, rather than having to depend on assumptions or intuition. For your A/B testing to work, you need to determine the criteria for success. For example, what is your hypothesis in this case? What do you think is going to happen by changing the images, call to action, and some of the keywords? Are you hoping to increase conversion rates? Get more newsletter signups? Determine your criteria for success ahead of time.

189

- **There's No Relevancy** - If your content is relevant to your audience, you're more likely to get the results that you want. Relevancy is the key. What you are trying to tell your audience has match what they want to hear. You have to make your audience *want* your product, to *long for it.* Create excitement within them so they can't wait to buy what you're selling. You also need to create content with some element of exclusivity incorporated into it and then boost it with your CTA. Tell your audience why they should buy from you and not your competitor. The more reasons you give them to want to purchase from you, the more they will stick around, especially if your CTA is compelling them to do so even more.

Some of the smallest details for a website, blog, email, or social media content are some of the most effective in changing perceptions, increasing conversion rates, and so on. Maybe the bright green call to action makes people become customers faster. By observing the other factors beyond your massive campaigns, you can discover that an A/B test has other impacts and effects that you were not anticipating. If those impressions were good, then you can focus your attention even more on them. If they are not good, then you might want to change it. Always remember that A/B testing can have larger implications than just the metrics alone.

This Is What a Call to Action SHOULD Be

A good call to action is so important for the success of your marketing campaigns. The question is, how do you build a good call to action? Let's break down the several ways to do that right now:

- **The Devil's in The Details -** All roads lead back to determining the exact details that your customers or your prospects truly want at the end of the day. When they come to your website or when they see one of your advertisements online, what do they truly want when they get to your landing page? What do they want to read about when they see an email from you? You need to give them the answers that they came looking for. Maybe they want information about pricing; maybe they want information, maybe they're looking for a specific product. You'll need to think about putting yourself in their shoes and try to understand what do they want most when they click through your content, and that needs to be the core of your call to action.

- **Made to Stand Out -** When you determine what your call to action is, you need to ensure it's suitable for all devices, whether it's a desktop or a mobile device. You want to make sure that your call to action is right there dominantly displayed. One good idea here is to make it a different color than everything else. That's called the call to action color, and that should carry throughout your copy so it's easy to identify with. If you have a long page of content, integrate that call to action throughout, so that the user constantly has it visible on the screen of their device, no matter where they are on the page.

- **Short and Sweet Will Do The Trick -** Keep it very concise, very short, and very sweet. It should literally fit be one button's worth of content and use keywords for urgency like *"now," "today."* Words like these will stand out to people and incentivize them to move forward quicker.

- **Consider Directional Cues** - Directional cues would be arrows. It could even be pictures near it with people pointing to your CTA. Those things might seem funny, but it helps steer your readers' eyes where you want it to go and to get somebody moving down the path a conversion.

- **Social Proof Near the CTA** - This could be the number of customers you've worked with your success stories, some of your review's statistics maybe some awards. Trust builds confidence and confidence leads to conversion so make sure that content is nearby your call to action to make it more persuasive for your readers.

- **It Leads to Your Landing Page** - Your copy should be leading to your landing page and it should be an exact match or aligned with your call to action. When they click on the link you've told them to in your email, they should literally see exactly the same thing on your landing page when they arrive there after clicking your call to action. Too often, marketers also make the mistake of having an ad copy that doesn't match their landing page or their call to action and those are wasted clicks.

- **Subtle Encouragement -** The best kind of CTA is one that encourages purchases in the right way. It's not too pushy; it's not too complacent, but just right. If the CTA does its job right, it should be placed near a highlighted benefit as a reminder to your readers that they could gain that same benefit too if they followed the CTA you were trying to get them to do. An exclusive, one-time offer or limited time offer could be thrown into the mix to sweeten the deal.

- **Ignites Curiosity** - Another thing a well-executed CTA does is to ignite curiosity and complement the written copy. Let's say you've already whetted the reader's appetite with your storytelling skills, in comes the CTA to give them that little nudge to find out more about what you've offered them. Encourage them to download that free eBook you've prepared just for them. Nudge them to find out more about what you've told them by visiting your website for more information.

- **Promise Something Specific** - Remember how vague details don't work? Well, with a CTA it's no different. Everything you send to your subscribers should deliver on what it promised, including the CTA. For example, if you promised them a free eBook that is going to answer all the questions they have and more, your CTA should deliver on that promise. People want the results they have been promised, and all it takes is just one time that they've felt they've been misled to turn them away from your business forever.

If you're not sure what best call to action to use, take a quick look at your competitors and see what it is they're doing that works well. Look at their landing pages and analyze what call to actions are they using and how are they using them. Take those ideas and implement them with your own creativity or better yet, see what you can do that is better than your competition. You don't need to reinvent the wheel; you only need to use what's working and what's already out there with common knowledge. That's a good way to get started.

The secret to great email marketing isn't that big of a secret at all. It merely boils down to understanding what works. Understanding how email marketing works, understanding how your target audience works, and understanding how these elements will work together to help your business get to the next level you're looking to accomplish. Not all marketing tools and techniques are going to be similar across the board. Each email copy you churn out needs to be as unique as your reader. Don't try to copy exactly what other businesses are doing, because not all businesses are the same. Each business needs to find a voice of their own. Email marketing is a world of variety and potential. But just like starting a new business, give yourself some time to learn the ropes. It may seem an overwhelming world to beginners because of how much information there is out there. If you're just starting out on your email marketing venture, give yourself time to learn. Do your market research and avoid making immensely costly mistakes.

No matter what, a compelling CTA is the result of the content that is high-quality and well-written.

If your readers are impressed by your email from start to finish, persuading them to take the desired next steps with your CTA is going to be no problem at all. In fact, they're more likely to follow through because they already enjoyed what you've told them so far in your email. Therefore, the entire email copywriting process needs to be a winner from start to finish. Every element that has been discussed throughout the book works together as a whole, each playing its part to create that final product, culminating in a call to action that ties it all together beautifully.

The end... almost!

Reviews are not easy to come by.

As an independent author with a tiny marketing budget, I rely on readers, like you, to leave a short review on Amazon.

Even if it's just a sentence or two!

So if you enjoyed the book, please...

>> Scan here to drop a brief review on Amazon.

I am very appreciative for your review as it truly makes a difference.

Thank you from the bottom of my heart for purchasing this book and reading it to the end.

Conclusion

Email marketing. A simple yet powerful tool capable of bringing tremendous results when used correctly. Copywriting, combined with the right marketing strategies, are the winning formula you need to set you on the path to success. You've uncovered within this book a deeper understanding of how significant email marketing and copywriting is for your business. If you are serious about increasing your revenue, *you must have email marketing* as part of your overall marketing measures.

The marketing world has made tremendous leaps and bounds over the years. It has certainly come a long way from the days of traditional print and old-school media ads. There's certainly no shortage of digital strategies to choose from, and despite the new up and coming trends that will no doubt present themselves in the years to come, email marketing is not going anywhere anytime soon. Don't put your business at risk of losing customers by getting caught up in all the other latest digital trends and overlook email marketing. Email marketing campaigns are designed to turn those cold leads into warm leads, and it works every time, which means that email marketing will always be a relevant necessity for every marketer and business, both big and small. It is a proven way to build trust with existing customers and prospective customers by moving the business conversation to a personal level, which is direct to your customer's inbox.

Email marketing and copywriting takes practice to perfect it, and as long as you stick to the following basic rules to go by, you can't go wrong:

- Always create a segmented and niche list for more specific targeting
- Use actionable words for your CTAs
- Define the purpose of your email with a well-written subject line

- Write opening sentences that are going to have them hooked from the start
- Stay away from trigger words that will put you at risk of getting marked as spam
- Focus on sticking to the best practices when it comes to writing your copy
- Craft CTAs that will guarantee results

Finally, remember that without great copywriting, your emails are nothing more than just meaningless eye candy to your readers. Email marketing campaigns are an extension of your overall marketing.

Resources:

14 Welcome Email Examples That Build Trust With Subscribers. (2020). Retrieved 2 May 2020, from https://optinmonster.com/welcome-email-examples-that-build-trust-with-subscribers/) [Accessed 27 April 2020].

30 Email Opening Lines That You Can Steal to Drive Engagement. (n.d.). Available at https://www.bluleadz.com/blog/email-opening-lines-that-will-instantly-hook-your-prospects [Retrieved May 3, 2020]

Allana Akhtar, Á. C. (2019, August 7). 18 tips for writing an excellent subject line so your email gets read. Available at https://www.businessinsider.com/how-to-write-an-email-subject-line-2015-1 [Retrieved May 3, 2020]

Allen, O. (n.d.). 19 Tips to Write Catchy Email Subject Lines [Examples]. Available at https://blog.hubspot.com/marketing/improve-your-email-subject-line [Accessed 27 April 2020].

Boogaard, K. (2020, February 24). 40 Email Opening Lines That Are So Much Better Than

"Happy Monday!" Available at
https://www.themuse.com/advice/40-better-
email-greetings-to-use-than-happy-monday
[Retrieved May 3, 2020]

Brudner, E. (n.d.). 25 Email Opening Lines and
Greetings That Put "Hi, My Name Is" to Shame.
Available at
https://blog.hubspot.com/sales/sales-email-
opening-lines [Retrieved May 3, 2020]

Brook, M. (2018, May 23). The Worst Email
Openings To Avoid (And What They Really
Mean). Available at
https://thecusp.com.au/worst-email-openings-
avoid-really-mean/20875 [Retrieved May 3,
2020]

Fernandez, M. (2020, April 23). (Updated) 164
Best Email Subject Lines to Boost Open Rates in
2020. Available at from
https://optinmonster.com/101-email-subject-
lines-your-subscribers-cant-resist/ [Retrieved
May 3, 2020]

Create a Website. (n.d.). Retrieved from
https://www.quicksprout.com/list-building/
[Accessed 27 April 2020].

Campaignmonitor.com. 2020. *Email List Building in The New Era of Email Marketing.* [online] Available at: https://www.campaignmonitor.com/resources/guides/email-list-building-new-era-email-marketing/ [Accessed 27 April 2020].

Campaignmonitor.com. 2020. *Email List Building In The New Era Of Email Marketing.* [online] Available at: https://www.campaignmonitor.com/resources/guides/email-list-building-new-era-email-marketing/ [Accessed 2 May 2020].
Campaign Monitor. (n.d.). 75 CTAs Your Next Email Campaign Needs (Updated). Available at https://www.campaignmonitor.com/blog/email-marketing/2019/03/75-call-to-actions-to-use-in-email-marketing-campaigns/ [Retrieved May 3, 2020].

Campaign Monitor. (n.d.). 8 Email Copywriting Tips for Engaging Content [+ Examples]. Available at https://www.campaignmonitor.com/blog/email-marketing/2018/11/8-email-copywriting-tips-for-engaging-content/ [Retrieved May 3, 2020].

Campaign Monitor. (n.d.-b). 10 Tips to Optimize Your Calls to Action in Email and Web. Available

at
https://www.campaignmonitor.com/resources/g
uides/10-tips-improve-email-calls-action/
[Retrieved May 3, 2020].

Cattoni, A. (2020, February 5). 4 Proven Email
Copywriting Templates. Available at
https://www.alexcattoni.com/4-proven-email-
copywriting-templates/ [Retrieved May 3, 2020].

Digital Marketing Blog. 2020. *Top 6 Reasons
Why Email Marketing Is A Must Have For Small
Businesses*. [online] Available at:
https://www.lyfemarketing.com/blog/why-email-
marketing [Accessed 2 May 2020].

Fernandez, M. (2020, April 23). (Updated) 164
Best Email Subject Lines to Boost Open Rates in
2020. Available at
https://optinmonster.com/101-email-subject-
lines-your-subscribers-cant-resist/ [Retrieved
May 3, 2020].

Gotter, A. (2019, September 10). 12 Fast Email
Copywriting Tips That Will Boost Your
Conversion Rates. Available at
https://www.disruptiveadvertising.com/email-
marketing/email-copywriting/ [Retrieved May 3,
2020].

Forsey, C. (n.d.). How to Build an Email List from Scratch: 10 Incredibly Effective Strategies. Retrieved from https://blog.hubspot.com/marketing/list-building

Forsey, C., 2020. *The Ultimate List of Email Marketing Stats For 2020*. [online] Blog.hubspot.com. Available at: https://blog.hubspot.com/marketing/email-marketing-stats [Accessed 27 April 2020].

Haden, J. (2018, February 20). 11 First Sentences That Guarantee the Rest of Your Email Won't Get Read. Available at https://www.inc.com/jeff-haden/11-first-sentences-that-guarantee-rest-of-your-email-wont-get-read.html [Retrieved May 3, 2020].

Hall, S. H. (2020, January 31). 17 Tips for Writing Email Marketing Copy that Converts. Available at https://optinmonster.com/9-tips-for-writing-email-marketing-copy-that-converts/ [Retrieved May 3, 2020].

Hexton, C. (2015, February 20). 5 Ways To Put Your Email Call To Action To Work. Available from https://marketingland.com/5-examples-of-how-to-put-your-email-call-to-action-to-work-48677 [Retrieved May 3, 2020].

Hussain, A., 2020. *22 Eye-Opening Statistics About Sales Email Subject Lines That Affect Open Rates [Updated For 2020].* [online] Blog.hubspot.com. Available at: https://blog.hubspot.com/sales/subject-line-stats-open-rates-slideshare [Accessed 27 April 2020].

How to Build Your Email List in Less than an Hour |. (n.d.). Available at https://mailchimp.com/resources/how-to-build-your-email-list/ [Retrieved May 3, 2020].

How You Can Build an Email Marketing List as Quickly as Possible. (n.d.). Available at https://neilpatel.com/blog/quick-email-marketing-lists/ [Retrieved May 3, 2020].

Jenkins, J. B. (2019, September 26). 249 Strong Verbs That'll Spice Up Your... Available at https://jerryjenkins.com/powerful-verbs/ [Retrieved May 3, 2020].

Kolowich, L. (n.d.). How to Write a Marketing Email: 10 Tips for Writing Compelling Email Copy. Available at https://blog.hubspot.com/blog/tabid/6307/bid/3 2606/The-9-Must-Have-Components-of-Compelling-Email-Copy.aspx [Retrieved May 3, 2020].

Kruse, K., 2020. *The 80/20 Rule and How It Can Change Your Life*. [online] Forbes. Available at: https://www.forbes.com/sites/kevinkruse/2016/ 03/07/80-20-rule/#41c88c573814 [Accessed 27 April 2020].

List Building 101: How to Build an Email List......And Actually Make Money From It. (n.d.). Retrieved from https://socialtriggers.com/list-building/ [Retrieved May 3, 2020].

Manifest, T. (2018, April 27). 8 Call to Action Examples for Email Marketing - The Manifest. Available at https://medium.com/@the_manifest/8-call-to-action-examples-for-email-marketing-e6804d965d4f [Retrieved May 3, 2020].

Medium. 2020. *The Jam Experiment — How Choice Overloads Makes Consumers Buy Less*. [online] Available at: https://medium.com/@FlorentGeerts/the-jam-experiment-how-choice-overloads-makes-consumers-buy-less-d610f8c37b9b [Accessed 27 April 2020].

Muse, T. (2020, February 6). 40 Different Email Greetings You Can Use in Your Next Message. Available at https://www.inc.com/the-muse/email-greeting-alternatives-options.html [Accessed 2 May 2020].

OptinMonster. 2020. *Why You Need To Build An Email List Right Now – And How To Get Started.* [online] Available at: https://optinmonster.com/why-you-need-to-build-an-email-list-right-now-and-the-exact-steps-on-how-to-get-started/ [Accessed 2 May 2020].

Ovient, Inc. (2015, May 2). 20 Sentences and Phrases for Beginning an Email. Available at https://www.ovient.com/resources/20-sentences-and-phrases-for-beginning-an-email/ [Accessed 2 May 2020].

Paquet, M. (2020, February 20). What is a Good Email Subject Line? Available at https://blogs.constantcontact.com/good-email-subject-lines/ [Retrieved May 3, 2020].

Pitre, A. (n.d.). 29 Simple Ways to Grow Your Email List Available at https://blog.hubspot.com/blog/tabid/6307/bid/3 2028/25-clever-ways-to-grow-your-email-marketing-list.aspx [Retrieved May 3, 202].

Radicati.com. 2020. [online] Available at: https://www.radicati.com/wp/wp-content/uploads/2015/02/Email-Statistics-Report-2015-2019-Executive-Summary.pdf [Accessed 27 April 2020].

Radicati.com. 2020. [online] Available at: https://radicati.com/wp/wp-content/uploads/2015/02/Email-Statistics-Report-2015-2019-Executive-Summary.pdf [Accessed 2 May 2020].

Pitre, A. (n.d.). 29 Simple Ways to Grow Your Email List. Available at https://blog.hubspot.com/blog/tabid/6307/bid/3 2028/25-clever-ways-to-grow-your-email-marketing-list.aspx Retrieved May 3, 202].

Santora, J. (2019, September 3). 12 Easy Ways To Build Your Free Email List Right Now. Available at from https://optinmonster.com/free-email-list/ [Retrieved May 3, 2020].

Search Engine Journal. 2020. *Email Marketing 101: How To Segment Your List - Search Engine Journal.* [online] Available at: https://www.searchenginejournal.com/email-marketing-101-how-to-segment-your-list/62606/ [Accessed 2 May 2020].

Sumo Group, Inc. (n.d.). 9 Common Call To Action Mistakes You Need To Avoid. Available at https://sumo.com/stories/call-to-action-mistakes [Accessed 2 May 2020].

Swiped.co. 2020. *$2 Billion Wall St. Journal Letter ("Tale of Two Young Men") By Martin Conroy » Swipe File Archive » Marketing & Copywriting Examples.* [online] Available at: https://swiped.co/file/wallstreet-letter-conroy/ [Accessed 27 April 2020].

Taylor, V. (2019, May 1). 23 Email Copywriting Tips to Skyrocket Conversions. Available at https://blog.wishpond.com/post/115675437806/email-copywriting [Accessed 2 May 2020].

The 9 Best Email Subject Line Styles to Increase Your Open Rates. (n.d.). Available at https://www.wordstream.com/blog/ws/2014/03/31/email-subject-lines [Accessed 2 May 2020].

The Daily Egg. 2020. *How To Create A Killer Email List From Nothing (A Beginner's Guide).* [online] Available at: https://www.crazyegg.com/blog/killer-email-list/ [Accessed 2 May 2020].

W. (2019, May 14). 7 CTA Mistakes Killing Your Conversion Rate. Retrieved from https://blog.wishpond.com/post/93137519369/7-cta-mistakes-killing-your-conversion-rate [Accessed 2 May 2020].

Wpbeginner.com. 2020. [online] Available at: https://www.wpbeginner.com/beginners-guide/why-you-should-start-building-your-email-list-right-away/ [Accessed 2 May 2020].